Microsoft® Office Outlook® 2010

Level 2

Microsoft® Office Outlook® 2010: Level 2

Part Number: 084596
Course Edition: 1.0

NOTICES

DISCLAIMER: While Element K Corporation takes care to ensure the accuracy and quality of these materials, we cannot guarantee their accuracy, and all materials are provided without any warranty whatsoever, including, but not limited to, the implied warranties of merchantability or fitness for a particular purpose. The name used in the data files for this course is that of a fictitious company. Any resemblance to current or future companies is purely coincidental. We do not believe we have used anyone's name in creating this course, but if we have, please notify us and we will change the name in the next revision of the course. Element K is an independent provider of integrated training solutions for individuals, businesses, educational institutions, and government agencies. Use of screenshots, photographs of another entity's products, or another entity's product name or service in this book is for editorial purposes only. No such use should be construed to imply sponsorship or endorsement of the book by, nor any affiliation of such entity with Element K. This courseware may contain links to sites on the Internet that are owned and operated by third parties (the "External Sites"). Element K is not responsible for the availability of, or the content located on or through, any External Site. Please contact Element K if you have any concerns regarding such links or External Sites.

TRADEMARK NOTICES Element K and the Element K logo are trademarks of Element K Corporation and its affiliates.

Outlook® 2010 is a registered trademark of Microsoft Corporation in the U.S. and other countries; the Microsoft products and services discussed or described may be trademarks of Microsoft Corporation. All other product names and services used throughout this course may be common law or registered trademarks of their respective proprietors.

Copyright © 2010 Element K Corporation. All rights reserved. Screenshots used for illustrative purposes are the property of the software proprietor. This publication, or any part thereof, may not be reproduced or transmitted in any form or by any means, electronic or mechanical, including photocopying, recording, storage in an information retrieval system, or otherwise, without express written permission of Element K, 500 Canal View Boulevard, Rochester, NY 14623, (585) 240-7500, (800) 478-7788. Element K Courseware's World Wide Web site is located at **www.elementkcourseware.com**.

This book conveys no rights in the software or other products about which it was written; all use or licensing of such software or other products is the responsibility of the user according to terms and conditions of the owner. Do not make illegal copies of books or software. If you believe that this book, related materials, or any other Element K materials are being reproduced or transmitted without permission, please call (800) 478-7788.

HELP US IMPROVE OUR COURSEWARE
Your comments are important to us. Please contact us at Element K Press LLC, 1-800-478-7788, 500 Canal View Boulevard, Rochester, NY 14623, Attention: Product Planning, or through our Web site at **http://support.elementkcourseware.com**.

Microsoft® Office Outlook® 2010: Level 2

Lesson 1: Customizing Message Options

- A. Modify Message Settings 2
- B. Modify Delivery Options 10
- C. Change the Message Format 15
- D. Set the Out of Office Notification 19
- E. Create a Contact Group 27
- F. Insert a Hyperlink 34
- G. Create Quick Steps 37

Lesson 2: Organizing and Locating Messages

- A. Sort Messages Using Multiple Criteria 44
- B. Find Messages Using Instant Search 48
- C. Find Messages Using Multiple Criteria 54
- D. Filter Messages 62
- E. Organize Messages 67
- F. Manage Junk Email 83

Lesson 3: Setting Calendar Options

- A. Set Workdays and Time 92
- B. Display an Additional Time Zone 97
- C. Set Availability Options 101
- D. Create Calendar Groups 105
- E. Manage Automatic Meeting Responses 107

Lesson 4: Tracking Activities Using the Journal

- A. Record a Journal Entry Automatically 114

Microsoft® Office Outlook® 2010: Level 2

    B. Record a Journal Entry Manually **119**

    C. Modify a Journal Entry.. **123**

Lesson 5: Managing Tasks

    A. Assign a Task **128**

    B. Reply to a Task Request **134**

    C. Send a Task Update **139**

    D. Track Assigned Tasks **142**

Lesson 6: Sharing Folder Information

    A. Specify Folder Permissions **148**

    B. Access Another User's Folder **154**

    C. Send Calendar Information in an Email Message **158**

    D. Delegate Folder Access to Users **162**

Lesson 7: Customizing the Outlook Environment

    A. Customize the Ribbon and Quick Access Toolbar **172**

    B. Customize the To-Do Bar..................................... **179**

    C. Create a Folder Home Page................................... **183**

Lesson Labs... **189**

Solutions **197**

Glossary **201**

Index **203**

About This Course

If you have been using Microsoft® Office Outlook® 2010 as a communications tool, then you know how to send a email message; schedule appointments and meetings; and create contacts, tasks, and notes. Now, you need to customize the settings such that you can incorporate your preferences in all the items. In this course, you will customize the Outlook environment, calendar, emails, and folders, and will also track, share, assign, and quickly locate various Outlook items.

Perhaps you want to keep track of your work activities using the Outlook Journal or customize your calendar, your email messages, or your Outlook environment to meet your specifications. You may also want to share Outlook items with other users or quickly locate or identify items within a large group of items. This course will show you how to perform these activities and more!

Course Description

Target Student

This course is designed for experienced Outlook users who need to customize their Outlook environment, calendar, and email messages and who wish to track, share, assign, and locate various Outlook items.

Course Prerequisites

Prospective students should be familiar with using personal computers (basic typing skills are recommended). They should be comfortable with the Windows environment and be able to use Windows to manage information on the computer. Specifically, they should be able to launch and close programs; navigate to information stored on the computer; and manage files and folders. Before taking this course, it is recommended that students take the following Element K courses or possess equivalent knowledge of Microsoft Office Outlook 2010: Level 1, and a choice of operating systems. Prerequisite courses include:

- *Windows XP Professional: Level 1*
- *Windows XP Professional: Level 2*

Course Objectives

In this course, you will customize the Outlook environment, calendar, and mail messages, and will also track, share, assign, and quickly locate various Outlook items.

You will:

- Customize message settings.
- Organize and locate Outlook messages.
- Set calendar options.
- Track activities using the Journal.
- Assign and track tasks.
- Share folder information.
- Customize the Outlook environment.

How to Use This Book

As a Learning Guide

This book is divided into lessons and topics, covering a subject or a set of related subjects. In most cases, lessons are arranged in order of increasing proficiency.

The results-oriented topics include relevant and supporting information you need to master the content. Each topic has various types of activities designed to enable you to practice the guidelines and procedures as well as to solidify your understanding of the informational material presented in the course.

At the back of the book, you will find a glossary of the definitions of the terms and concepts used throughout the course. You will also find an index to assist in locating information within the instructional components of the book.

In the Classroom

This book is intended to enhance and support the in-class experience. Procedures and guidelines are presented in a concise fashion along with activities and discussions. Information is provided for reference and reflection in such a way as to facilitate understanding and practice.

Each lesson may also include a Lesson Lab or various types of simulated activities. You will find the files for the simulated activities along with the other course files on the enclosed CD-ROM. If your course manual did not come with a CD-ROM, please go to **http://elementkcourseware.com** to download the files. If included, these interactive activities enable you to practice your skills in an immersive business environment, or to use hardware and software resources not available in the classroom. The course files that are available on the CD-ROM or by download may also contain sample files, support files, and additional reference materials for use both during and after the course.

As a Teaching Guide

Effective presentation of the information and skills contained in this book requires adequate preparation. As such, as an instructor, you should familiarize yourself with the content of the entire course, including its organization and approaches. You should review each of the student activities and exercises so you can facilitate them in the classroom.

Throughout the book, you may see Instructor Notes that provide suggestions, answers to problems, and supplemental information for you, the instructor. You may also see references to "Additional Instructor Notes" that contain expanded instructional information; these notes appear in a separate section at the back of the book. PowerPoint slides may be provided on the included course files, which are available on the enclosed CD-ROM or by download from http://elementkcourseware.com. The slides are also referred to in the text. If you plan to use the slides, it is recommended to display them during the corresponding content as indicated in the instructor notes in the margin.

The course files may also include assessments for the course, which can be administered diagnostically before the class, or as a review after the course is completed. These exam-type questions can be used to gauge the students' understanding and assimilation of course content.

As a Review Tool

Any method of instruction is only as effective as the time and effort you, the student, are willing to invest in it. In addition, some of the information that you learn in class may not be important to you immediately, but it may become important later. For this reason, we encourage you to spend some time reviewing the content of the course after your time in the classroom.

As a Reference

The organization and layout of this book make it an easy-to-use resource for future reference. Taking advantage of the glossary, index, and table of contents, you can use this book as a first source of definitions, background information, and summaries.

Course Icons

Icon	Description
	A **Caution Note** makes students aware of potential negative consequences of an action, setting, or decision that are not easily known.
	Display Slide provides a prompt to the instructor to display a specific slide. Display Slides are included in the Instructor Guide only.
	An **Instructor Note** is a comment to the instructor regarding delivery, classroom strategy, classroom tools, exceptions, and other special considerations. Instructor Notes are included in the Instructor Guide only.
	Notes Page indicates a page that has been left intentionally blank for students to write on.
	A **Student Note** provides additional information, guidance, or hints about a topic or task.
	A **Version Note** indicates information necessary for a specific version of software.

Course Requirements and Setup

You can find a list of hardware and software requirements to run this class as well as detailed classroom setup procedures in the course files that are available on the CD-ROM that shipped with this book. If your course manual did not come with a CD-ROM, please go to **http://www.elementk.com/courseware-file-downloads** to download the files.

1 Customizing Message Options

Lesson Time: 1 hour(s), 50 minutes

Lesson Objectives:

In this lesson, you will customize message settings.

You will:

- Modify message settings.
- Modify delivery options.
- Change the message format.
- Notify others that you will be out of office.
- Create a contact group.
- Insert a hyperlink.
- Create a quick step.

Introduction

You explored the Microsoft Office Outlook user interface and performed some basic tasks using mail default forms and settings. Additionally, you worked with basic calendar and contacts features. Now, you may want to adapt the Outlook email feature to suit your needs. In this lesson, you will customize your message by changing the message settings.

You may find that you are sending routine email messages to clients and coworkers that do not always warrant the same level of attention or importance as some messages do. Outlook provides you with a variety of message options that enable you to alert recipients to a message's importance and sensitivity.

TOPIC A
Modify Message Settings

You have experience in sending email messages using Outlook. Although most of your messages may not always need special attention and handling, but you may have, at times, found the need to inform the recipients of the importance and sensitivity of email messages. In this topic, you will modify message settings so that you can mark your messages for special attention and handling.

As an Outlook user, you routinely send and receive email. The importance and sensitivity of the messages you send varies. Perhaps you may want to send a message to your manager that requires her immediate attention and the same message contains confidential information. To inform the recipient of how to handle your message, you must know how to modify message settings. Outlook enables you to modify message settings and make email messages stand out and call attention to the recipient.

Message Settings

Message settings are used to specify the importance and sensitivity of a message. There are various **Importance** and **Sensitivity** options that you can modify as needed. The importance of a message is indicated by an icon located beside the message icon in the **Inbox**. The InfoBar displays both the sensitivity and importance of a message.

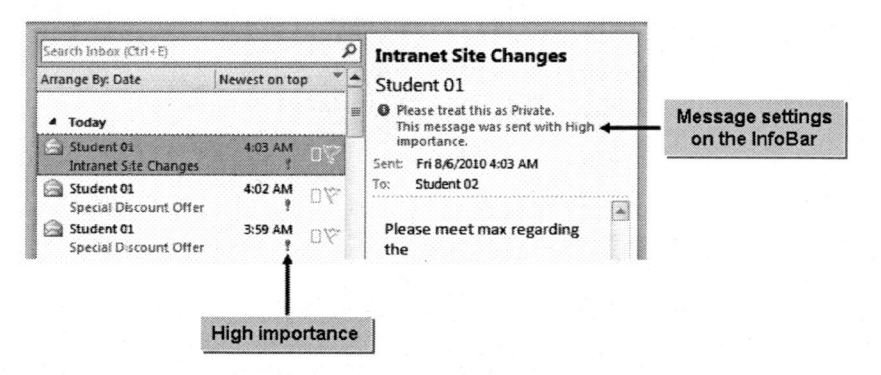

Figure 1-1: A message marked private and highly important.

Types of Message Settings
Outlook provides you with different message settings.

Setting	Options
Importance	• Low
	• Normal
	• High
Sensitivity	• Normal
	• Personal
	• Private
	• Confidential

Voting Buttons

Email messages are often used to gather information or to obtain feedback. Outlook's **Voting and Tracking options** allow you to create voting buttons within an email message that give the recipient the option of responding to a question just by clicking the appropriate button.

You can create your own custom voting buttons or use one of the three standard Outlook voting buttons.

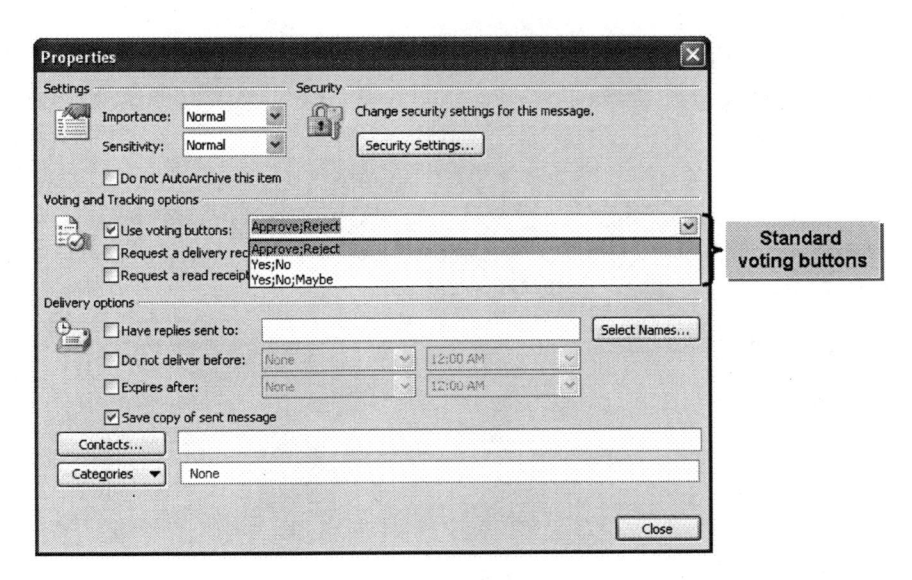

Figure 1-2: The list of standard voting buttons in the Properties dialog box.

Button Type	Description
Standard voting buttons	These are voting buttons that are available by default. Outlook provides three standard voting buttons: • **Approve;Reject** —Can be used when you need authorization. • **Yes;No**—Can be used for a quick poll where the response is either yes or no. • **Yes;No;Maybe**—Can be used when you do not wish to restrict responses to only yes and no answers.
Custom voting buttons	These are the voting buttons that you can create according to your needs and preferences.

How to Modify Message Settings

Procedure Reference: Modify Message Settings

To modify message settings:

1. Open a new Message window.
2. On the **Message** tab, in the **Tags** group, click the Dialog Box Launcher button to open the **Properties** dialog box.
3. In the **Settings** section, from the **Importance** drop-down list, select the desired option: **Low, Normal,** or **High.**
4. From the **Sensitivity** drop-down list, select the desired option: **Normal, Personal, Private,** or **Confidential.**
5. Click **Close.**
6. In the Message window toolbar, a square frame is displayed around the selected importance symbol. Information about the importance and sensitivity will also be displayed in an InfoBar when the recipient opens the message.

> You can also use the buttons on the Message window toolbar to set High or Low importance.

Procedure Reference: Forward a Message Without the High Importance Flag

To forward a message without the high importance flag:

1. Double-click the message marked as important, that you want to forward.
2. On the **Message** tab, in the **Tags** group, click the Dialog Box Launcher button to open the **Properties** dialog box.
3. In the **Settings** section, from the **Importance** drop-down list, select **Normal** and click **Close.**
4. Observe that the high importance symbol has been removed from the message.
5. On the **Message** tab, in the **Respond** group, click **Forward.**
6. Address the message to your partner and click **Send.**

Procedure Reference: Create a Message with Voting Buttons

To create a message with voting buttons:

1. Open a new Message window.
2. On the **Message** tab, in the **Tags** group, click the Dialog Box Launcher button to open the **Properties** dialog box.
3. In the **Voting and Tracking options** section, check the **Use voting buttons** check box.
4. From the **Use voting buttons** drop-down list, select the desired option or replace the default option in the text box with your custom voting options, separating each option with a semicolon.
5. Click **Close.**

> The buttons will not be displayed until the message is sent.

ACTIVITY 1-1
Modifying Message Settings

Setup:
The Outlook window is displayed.

Scenario:
You need to send an urgent email message to a client who requires a reply within 24 hours. The message contains confidential information about a discount that you are offering to this customer only. You not only need this message to stand out in your client's Inbox but also want to make certain that she does not relay the offer information to anyone else. Also, your manager has requested that you forward him a copy of this email. Because the email is just for your manager's reference, you decide to remove the High Importance symbol before forwarding it to him.

Student 01

1. Create a new message with high importance and confidential sensitivity.

    a. Display the **Inbox** folder.

    b. On the **Home** tab, click **New E-mail** to open a new Message window.

    c. On the **Message** tab, in the **Tags** group, click the Dialog Box Launcher button to open the **Properties** dialog box.

    d. In the **Settings** section, from the **Importance** drop-down list, select **High**.

    e. From the **Sensitivity** drop-down list, select **Confidential** and click **Close**.

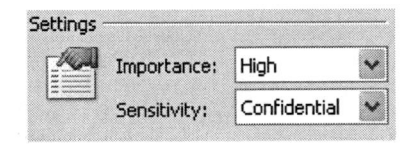

    f. Observe that the **High Importance** symbol is selected in the **Tags** group, indicating the level of importance of this message.

Student 01

2. Create and send a message.

   a. Create an email message addressed to your partner with the subject *Special Discount Offer!*

   b. In the message body, type *We would like to offer you a one time deal on the product that we discussed. Please reply within 24 hours if interested.*

   c. In the Message window, click **Send**.

Student 02

3. Check the message that you just received from your partner.

   a. Select the **Special Discount Offer!** message.

   b. Observe that the High Importance symbol is displayed after the subject in the Preview pane, and that the **Please treat this as confidential** and **This message was sent with high importance** messages are displayed in the InfoBar of the Reading pane.

   Special Discount Offer!

   Student 01

   ● Please treat this as Confidential.
   This message was sent with High importance.

   Sent: Tue 8/17/2010 1:28 PM
   To: Student 02

Student 01

4. Remove the High Importance symbol from a message before forwarding it.

    a. Display the **Sent Items** folder.

    b. Double-click the **Special Discount Offer!** message, to open it.

    c. On the **Message** tab, in the **Tags** group, click the Dialog Box Launcher button, to open the **Properties** dialog box.

    d. In the **Settings** section, from the **Importance** drop-down list, select **Normal** and click **Close.**

    e. Observe that the High Importance symbol has been removed from the message.

    f. On the **Message** tab, in the **Respond** group, click **Forward.**

    g. Address the message to your partner and click **Send.**

    h. Close the Message window.

    i. In the **Microsoft Outlook** message box, click **No.**

5. **True or False? You can view the message sensitivity level in the message InfoBar.**

    ___ True

    ___ False

6. **True or False? When you forward a message, you can remove the importance setting but not the sensitivity setting.**

    ___ True

    ___ False

ACTIVITY 1-2
Creating a Message with Voting Buttons

Scenario:
You have decided to subscribe to the Microsoft Office Online forum. You want to poll your team members to see if they would also be interested in joining the forum. Therefore, you decide to send an email with voting buttons so that you can quickly tabulate the voting results.

1. Create a message with standard voting buttons.

    a. On the **Home** tab, click **New E-mail** to open a new Message window.

    b. Address an email message to two of your partners with the subject **Please Vote**

    c. In the message body, type **Would you be interested in registering with the Microsoft Office Online forum?**

    d. On the **Message** tab, in the **Tags** group, click the Dialog Box Launcher button to display the **Properties** dialog box.

    e. In the **Voting and Tracking options** section, check the **Use voting buttons** check box.

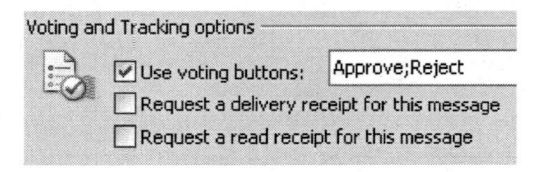

    f. From the **Use voting buttons** drop-down list, select **Yes;No** and click **Close**.

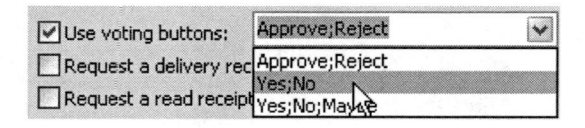

    g. Click **Send** to send the message.

2. Accept the message that you just received from your partner.

    a. Open the **Please Vote** message.

b. On the **Message** tab, in the **Respond** group, from the **Vote** drop-down list, select **Yes**.

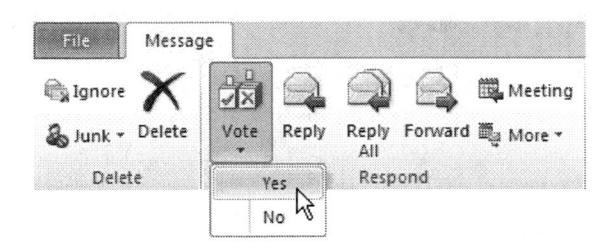

c. In the **Microsoft Outlook** warning box, click **OK** to send the response.

d. Close the Message window.

3. Reject the message that you just received from your partner.

   a. Open the **Please Vote** message.

   b. On the **Message** tab, in the **Respond** group, from the **Vote** drop-down list, select **No**.

   c. In the **Microsoft Outlook** warning box, click **OK** to send the response.

   d. Close the Message window.

4. Check the responses that you received from your partners.

   a. Open the **Yes: Please Vote** message.

   b. Observe that the **The sender responded: Yes** message appears on the InfoBar, indicating that the sender has accepted the request.

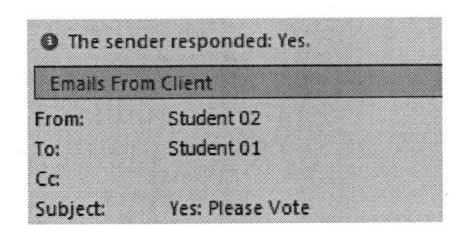

   c. Close the message window.

   d. Select the **No: Please Vote** message.

   e. Observe that the **The sender responded: No** message appears on the InfoBar, indicating that the sender has declined the request.

TOPIC B
Modify Delivery Options

You have informed recipients of how to handle messages by modifying message settings. When you send an email, you probably take it for granted that the message is sent out as soon as the **Send** button is clicked, that a copy of the message goes into the **Sent Items** folder, and that once the message is sent, it stays in the recipient's mailbox until the recipient decides to delete it. However, that does not always have to be the case. In this topic, you will modify delivery options.

Have you ever sent an email and eagerly waited for the recipient to reply, wondering whether the recipient has read the message or not? Or perhaps you have an email you want delivered on a schedule rather than sending it immediately. Outlook provides you with delivery options that allow you to perform such tasks by customizing the way your message is delivered.

Delivery Options

Delivery options enable you to change the way Outlook delivers your message. They also allow you to:

- Specify that replies have been sent to someone other than the sender of the message.
- Delay the delivery of the message until the specified date and time. Outlook stores the delayed message in the **Outbox** folder until it is delivered.
- Let the message expire after the specified date and time. If the recipient does not open the message before the expiration date and time, it is deleted. If the recipient opens the message, it is crossed out.

By default, Outlook saves the messages you send in the **Sent Items** folder. However, you can choose the location where you want a copy of your message to be saved, or choose not to save messages at all.

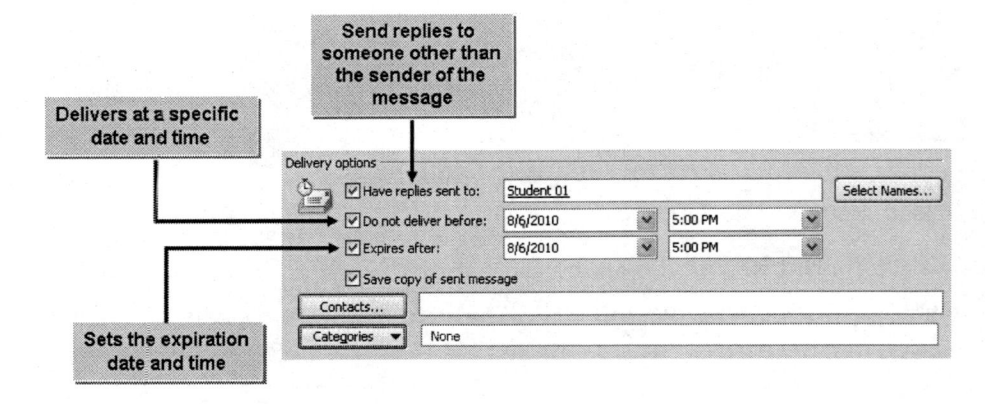

Figure 1-3: The various delivery options in the Properties dialog box.

Delivery Receipts

A *delivery receipt* is a message notification that confirms that your message was delivered to its intended recipients. You can request that Outlook send you a delivery receipt for either a particular message or for every email that you send. A delivery receipt gives you the email addresses of recipients and the date and time of delivery of the message. In the **Inbox,** a delivery receipt is indicated by an arrow enclosed by a circle. Outlook automatically records the contents of the delivery receipt notification in the original message in the **Sent Items** folder.

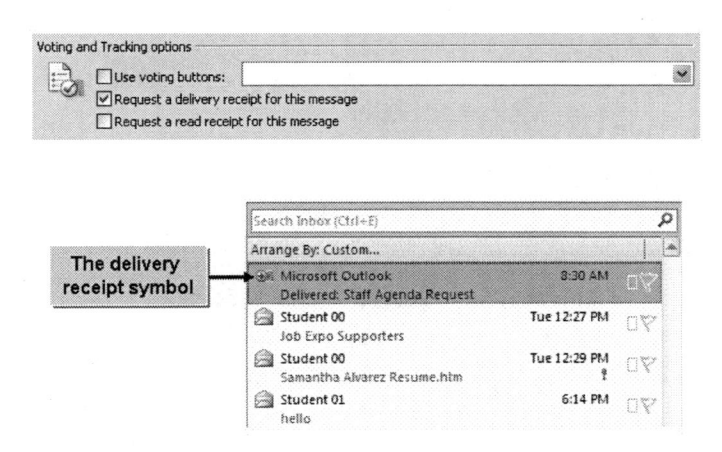

Figure 1-4: The delivery receipt message notification is set and the message is displayed in Inbox with the delivery receipt symbol.

Read Receipts

A *read receipt* is a message notification that confirms that the recipient has read your message. You can request that Outlook send you a read receipt for either a particular message or for every email you send. A read receipt gives you the email addresses of recipients and the date and time your message was read. In the **Inbox,** a read receipt is indicated by a tick mark enclosed by a circle. Outlook allows a recipient to deny a request for a read receipt, and if the recipient chooses to deny, the sender will not get a read receipt when the message is read. A message can have both a read receipt and a delivery receipt, and Outlook automatically records the contents of both notifications in the original message in the **Sent Items** folder.

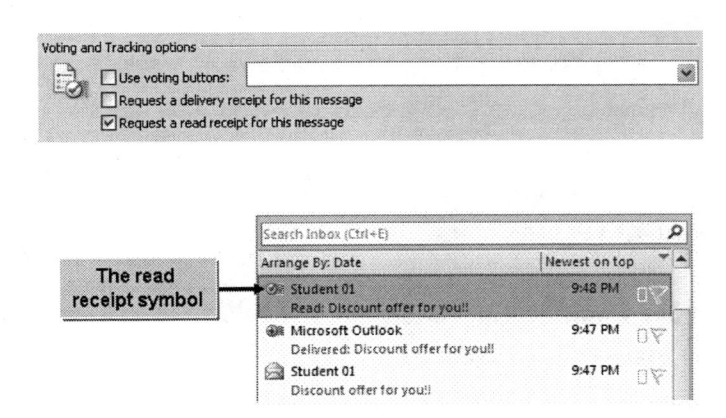

Figure 1-5: The read receipt message notification is set and the message is displayed in Inbox with the read receipt symbol.

How to Modify Delivery Options

Procedure Reference: Modify Delivery Options

To modify delivery options:

1. Open a Message window.
2. On the **Message** tab, in the **Tags** group, click the Dialog Box Launcher button to open the **Properties** dialog box.
3. If you want the message replies to go to someone other than yourself, specify to whom the replies should be sent.
    a. In the **Delivery options** section, check the **Have replies sent to** check box.
    b. Click **Select Names.**
    c. In the **Have Replies Sent To: Global Address List** dialog box, select the **Name only** option, and double-click the desired names.
    d. Click **OK** to close the dialog box.
4. Request a read receipt and a delivery receipt for the message.
    - In the **Voting and Tracking options** section, check the **Request a read receipt for this message** check box to be notified once the recipient has read your message.
    - In the **Voting and Tracking options** section, check the **Request a delivery receipt for this message** check box to be notified once the message was delivered.
5. If necessary, specify where the sent messages are to be saved.
    - Save copies of sent messages in the **Sent Items** folder.
        a. Open a Message window.
        b. On the **Options** tab, in the **More Options** group, from the **Save Sent Item To** drop-down list, select **Use Default Folder.** (This is the default option.)
    - From the **Save Sent Item To** drop-down list, select **Other Folder** and navigate to the desired folder to save copies somewhere other than the **Sent Items** folder.
    - If you do not want to keep copies of messages you send to others, from the **Save Sent Item To** drop-down list, select **Do Not Save.**
6. If you do not want the message delivered immediately, specify a delivery date and time.
    a. In the **Delivery options** section, check the **Do not deliver before** check box.
    b. From the first **Do not deliver before** drop-down list, select the desired delivery date from the calendar.
    c. From the second **Do not deliver before** drop-down list, select the delivery time.
7. If you want the message to expire on a specific date and time, specify an expiration date and time.
    a. In the **Delivery options** section, check the **Expires after** check box.
    b. From the first **Expires after** drop-down list, select the desired delivery date from the calendar.
    c. From the second **Expires after** drop-down list, select the delivery time.
8. Click **Close** to set the delivery options and close the dialog box.

Microsoft® Office Outlook® 2010: Level 2

ACTIVITY 1-3
Modifying Delivery Options

Scenario:
You need to solicit agenda items for an upcoming staff meeting. Because your assistant will create the agenda, you want replies to this message to go directly to him. To avoid confusion with a staff meeting occurring later that day, you do not want this message delivered until 8:30 the next day. You also want to confirm the delivery of the message to your assistant. Furthermore, you want to keep track of whether or not your assistant has read your message. Finally, to avoid any late feedback, you want the message to expire if unread within three days' time.

1. Create a new message addressed to your partner requesting agenda items.

    a. On the **Home** tab, in the **New** group, click **New E-mail** to open a new Message window.

    b. Create an email message to your partner with the subject **Staff Agenda Request** and the message **Please let me know if you have any items you would like to add to the agenda.**

2. Set the delivery option such that the replies are sent to you and your assistant.

    a. On the **Message** tab, in the **Tags** group, click the Dialog Box Launcher button to open the **Properties** dialog box.

    b. In the **Properties** dialog box, in the **Delivery options** section, check the **Have replies sent to** check box to specify to whom replies should be sent.

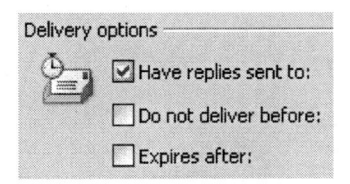

    c. In the **Delivery options** section, click **Select Names**.

    d. In the **Have Replies Sent To: Global Address List** dialog box, verify that the **Name only** option is selected, double-click your partner's name, and click **OK**.

3. Add a read receipt and a delivery receipt to the message.

    a. In the **Voting and Tracking options** section, check the **Request a delivery receipt for this message** check box to confirm the delivery of the message.

Lesson 1: Customizing Message Options   13

b. In the **Voting and Tracking options** section, check the **Request a read receipt for this message** check box to confirm that the recipient has read your message.

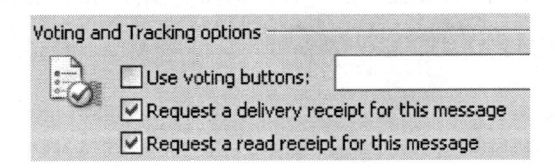

4. Set the message delivery time to 8:30 AM one day from the current date.

   a. In the **Delivery options** section, check the **Do not deliver before** check box.

   b. From the first **Do not deliver before** drop-down list, select the next working day from the calendar.

   c. From the second **Do not deliver before** drop-down list, select **8:30 AM.**

5. Set the message to expire at 5:30 PM after three working days from the original date.

   a. In the **Delivery options** section, check the **Expires after** check box.

   b. From the first **Expires after** drop-down list, in the calendar, select the third working day from today.

   c. From the second **Expires after** drop-down list, select **5:30 PM** and click **Close.**

   d. Click **Send.**

   > Open the Inbox to verify the notification email messages regarding the delivery and read receipts.

   e. In the Navigation pane, select the **Outbox** folder.

   f. Observe that the message is stored in the Outbox until the specified delivery date.

   g. Return to the **Inbox** folder.

TOPIC C
Change the Message Format

You have modified delivery options and customized the way your messages are delivered. Every recipient may not be able to receive messages in Outlook's default HTML format. In this topic, you will change the message format so that the messages are displayed in a different format.

The advantage of using Outlook's default HTML format for sending messages is the ability to use formatting and graphics, which can help convey your message more effectively. However, the email system of some customers may not support the HTML format, and they may be unable to read your messages. To ensure that every recipient is able to read your messages, you have the option to change the message format.

Message Formats

Definition:
A *message format* is a method of encoding an email that determines the formats that can be applied to a message and how the message is displayed. Three of the most commonly used message formats are the *HTML* format, *plain text* format, and *RTF* (Rich Text Format) format. HTML is Outlook's default message format. A message can include only those formatting features that the message format supports.

Example: Message Formats
This is how an HTML formatted message would appear.

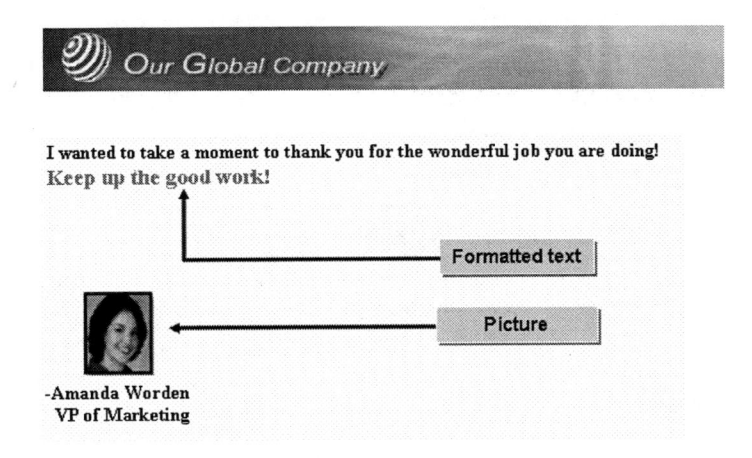

An HTML formatted message

Figure 1-6: An HTML formatted message.

This is how a plaintext formatted message would appear.

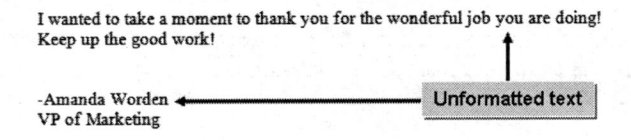

> I wanted to take a moment to thank you for the wonderful job you are doing!
> Keep up the good work!
>
> -Amanda Worden ← Unformatted text
> VP of Marketing

A plain text formatted message

Figure 1-7: A plain text formatted message.

This is how a rich text formatted message would appear.

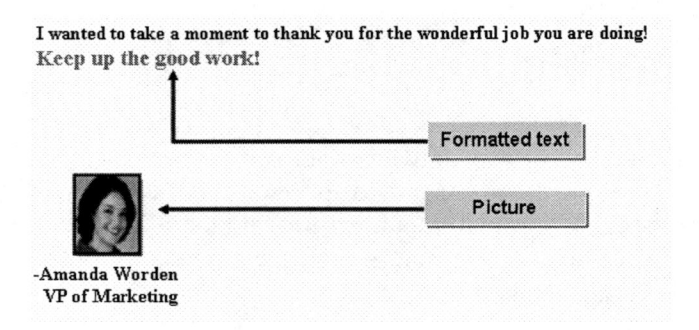

> I wanted to take a moment to thank you for the wonderful job you are doing!
> **Keep up the good work!** ← Formatted text
>
> [photo] ← Picture
> -Amanda Worden
> VP of Marketing

A rich text formatted message

Figure 1-8: A rich text formatted message.

Commonly Used Message Formats

The commonly used message formats are HTML, plaintext, and rich text format.

Message Format	What Is Displayed
Hypertext Markup Language (*HTML*)	Displays all text formatting, numbering, bullets, alignment, pictures, HTML styles, and hyperlinks. It is the recommended format for Internet email messages and messages sent using the Microsoft Exchange server.
Plain text	Displays only text. It does not support pictures, bold or italic formatting, colored fonts, and other text formatting. It can be read by all email programs.
Rich Text Format (*RTF*)	Displays text formatting, bullets, alignment, pictures, and linked objects. It can be read only using Microsoft Outlook and Microsoft Exchange.

How to Change the Message Format

Procedure Reference: Specify an Individual Message Format

To specify an individual message format:

1. If necessary, open a Message window.
2. On the **Format Text** tab, in the **Format** group, select the desired message format: **HTML, Rich Text,** or **Plain Text.**

> The default message format is HTML.

3. Enter the subject text and the message.
4. Send the message.

Procedure Reference: Modify the Default Message Format

To modify the default message format:

1. On the **File** tab, click **Options** to open the **Outlook Options** dialog box.
2. Select the **Mail** tab.
3. In the **Compose messages** section, from the **Compose message in this format** drop-down list, select the desired message format: **HTML, Rich Text,** or **.Plain Text.**
4. Click **OK.**

ACTIVITY 1-4
Specifying the Message Format

Scenario:

You need to inquire about some job requirements with one of your clients. Since the client uses an email system that does not support HTML format, he asks you to send messages using plaintext format.

1. Create a message, applying plaintext format.

    a. Create an email message to your partner with the subject **Job Requirements**

    b. On the **Format Text** tab, in the **Format** group, click **Aa Plain Text**.

    > When you create a message in Outlook, the default format is HTML.

    c. In the message body, type **Please provide me with your specific job requirements ASAP. Thanks.**

    d. Send the message.

    e. If necessary, in the **Microsoft Outlook Compatibility Check** dialog box, click **Continue**.

2. **True or False? In a Message window, text formatting options, such as bold and italic, are available on the Options tab.**

    ___ True

    ___ False

TOPIC D
Set the Out of Office Notification

You have changed the message format so that your recipients can read your messages. You can customize your messages even further by instructing Outlook to send specific messages on your behalf when you are out of office. In this topic, you will set a notification system that replies to anyone sending you mail and inform them of your absence.

Whenever you go on a vacation or you are out of town and unable to access your email, it is important to notify your coworkers and clients that you are out of office and not reading your emails. This is not only a courtesy, but it helps to avoid any potential communication problems. Outlook allows you to specify the actions that can be taken when someone tries to email you in your absence. This can include a brief statement directing people to contact your assistant, or other designated employee, with time-sensitive issues.

The Automatic Replies Dialog Box

The *Automatic Replies* dialog box allows you to specify automatic replies that will go back to anyone that sends you an email when you are out of the office. You can set the date and time that the message should be sent and also set the message to expire at a specified date and time. The **Inside My Organization** and **Outside My Organization** tabs allow you to specify the appropriate message you wish to communicate to each group. The option in the **Inside My Organization** tab sends your message only to people in your organization, and the option in the **Outside My Organization** tab sends your message to people outside your organization. The **Rules** option allows you to specify rules that will be applied to incoming messages when you are out of the office.

> The **Automatic Replies** dialog box was previously called the Out Of Office Assistant dialog box.

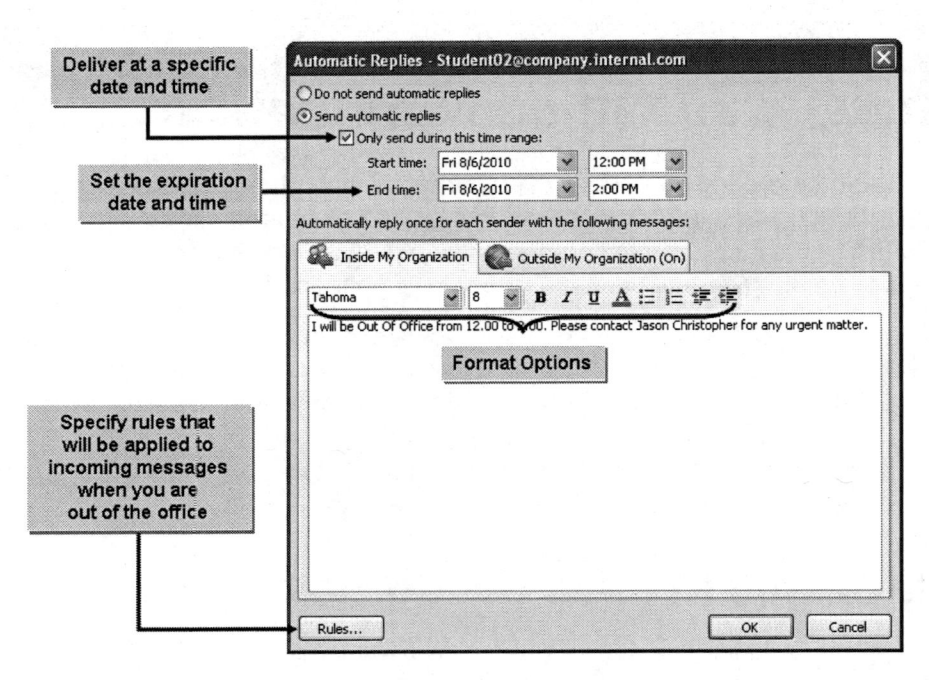

Figure 1-9: The Automatic Replies dialog box used to set Out of Office timings and messages.

Rules

Definition:
Rules are instructions that enable Outlook to perform specific tasks automatically, depending on the characteristics of a message. A *rule* is composed of a set of *conditions* that check the characteristics of a message and a set of *actions* that are to be performed when the conditions are met. Rules have different condition-action combinations.

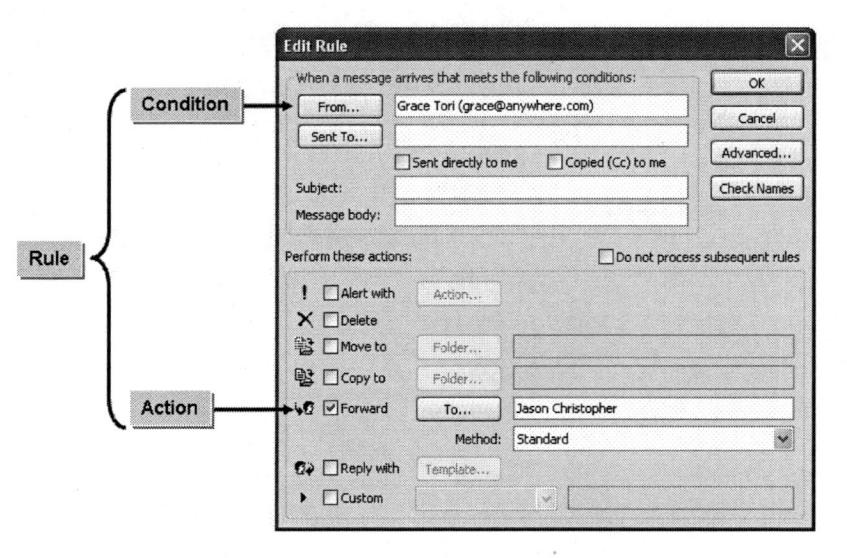

Figure 1-10: An Automatic Replies rule with a condition and an action.

Example: Automatic Replies Rules
Examples of conditions and actions that make up an Automatic Reply include:

Condition	Action
Messages received from a specified key client.	Forward email to assistant.
Messages about a current project.	Forward email to manager.
A routine daily update from a specified company.	Delete the email.
About a specified project.	Move message to the Project folder.

How to Set an Out of Office Notification

Procedure Reference: Set an Out of Office Notification

To notify others that you will be out of office:

1. On the **File** tab, click **Info.**
2. On the **Account Information** page, click **Automatic Replies.**
3. In the **Automatic Replies** dialog box, select the **Send automatic-replies** option.
4. On the **Inside My Organization** tab, in the message box, type the message you want people to receive.

> You can use the controls on the **Inside My Organization** and **Outside My Organization (On)** tabs to change the font, font size, and other text formatting as necessary.

5. Click **Rules** to display the **Automatic Reply Rules** dialog box.
6. Click **Add Rule** to apply additional rules.
7. In the **Edit Rule** dialog box, in the **When a message arrives that meets the following conditions** section, specify the conditions to be met.
8. In the **Perform these actions** section, specify what Outlook should do with messages that meet the conditions.
9. Click **OK** to close the **Edit Rule** dialog box.
10. Click **OK** to close the **Automatic Reply Rules** dialog box.
11. If necessary, set automatic messages to expire at a specified date and time.
    a. In the **Automatic Replies** dialog box, check the **Only send during this time range** check box.
    b. From the **End time** drop-down list, select the desired end date and time.
12. If necessary, on the **Outside My Organization (On)** tab, uncheck the **Auto-reply to people outside my organization** check box.
13. Click **OK** to close the **Automatic Replies** dialog box.
14. Observe that a message appears on the status bar indicating that the Out of Office auto-replies are turned on.

> When you return to the office, don't forget to turn off the **Automatic Replies**; otherwise, Outlook will continue to automatically reply to your incoming messages.

Procedure Reference: Turn off the Automatic Replies Feature

To turn off the Automatic replies feature:

1. On the status bar, select the **Automatic Replies** option.
2. In the **Automatic Replies** dialog box, select the **Do not send automatic replies** option.

Procedure Reference: Send External Out of Office Messages

To send external Out of Office messages to those who appear in your contacts:

> Ensure that you have contacts in your Contacts folder.

1. Display the **Automatic Replies** dialog box.
2. In the **Automatic Replies** dialog box, select the **Send automatic replies** option.
3. Select the **Outside My Organization (On)** tab.
4. If necessary, check the **Auto-reply to people outside my organization** check box to send auto-replies to people outside the organization.
5. Select the **My Contacts only** option to send an auto-reply only to people who are listed in your contacts.
6. If necessary, select the **Anyone outside my organization** option to send an auto-reply to each person who sends you an email message.

> The **Anyone Outside My Organization** option is selected by default.

7. On the **Outside My Organization (On)** tab, in the message box, type the message you want people to receive.
8. If necessary, set the messages to expire at a specified date and time.
9. Click **OK** to apply the changes.

ACTIVITY 1-5
Notifying Others That You Are Out of Office

Scenario:
You are going out of town for a week and need to notify anyone, who may try to contact you through email, of your absence. You also want to notify them that they can contact your assistant, Jason Christopher, for any urgent matters. Additionally, you're expecting an immediate reply from a client, Grace Tori, that must be forwarded to your assistant upon arrival. After getting back, you want to direct the future messages back to yourself and therefore delete the rule.

Student 01

1. Create an out of office message.

    a. Select the **File** tab.

    b. On the **Account Information** page, click **Automatic Replies.**

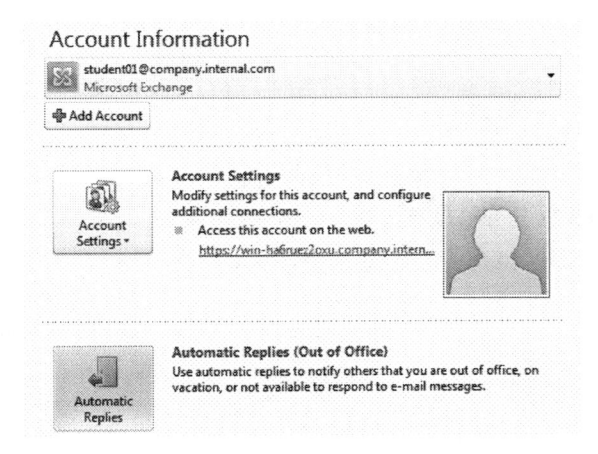

    c. In the **Automatic Replies** dialog box, select the **Send automatic replies** option.

    d. On the **Inside My Organization** tab, in the message box, type *Please contact Jason Christopher for any urgent matters.*

Student 01

2. When a message arrives from the specified client, have it forwarded to your assistant.

   a. In the **Automatic Replies** dialog box, click **Rules.**

   b. In the **Automatic Reply Rules** dialog box, click **Add Rule** to apply additional rules.

   c. In the **Edit Rule** dialog box, in the **When a message arrives that meets the following conditions** section, click **From** to display the **Choose Sender** dialog box.

   d. In the **Name** list, double-click the name of your partner and click **OK.**

   e. In the **Edit Rule** dialog box, verify that the name you selected is displayed in the **From** text box.

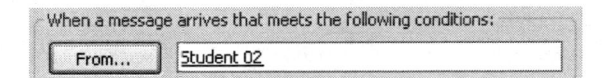

   f. In the **Perform these actions** section, check the **Forward** check box.

   g. Next to the **Forward** check box, click **To** to display the **Choose Recipient** dialog box.

   h. In the **Name** list, double-click the name of your third partner to add this name to the **To** text box and click **OK.**

   i. Verify that the name of the person you have selected to forward the email to is displayed in the **To** text box.

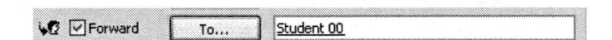

   j. Click **OK** to close the **Edit Rule** dialog box.

   k. Click **OK** to close the **Automatic Reply Rules** dialog box.

Student 01

3. Set Out of Office messages to expire at a specified time.

    a. In the **Automatic Replies** dialog box, check the **Only send during this time range** check box.

    b. From the first **End time** drop-down list, select the second working day from today to specify the expiration date.

    c. From the second **End Time** drop-down list, select the desired time to specify the expiration time.

    d. Select the **Outside My Organization (On)** tab.

    e. Uncheck the **Auto-reply to people outside my organization** check box and click **OK**.

    f. Select the **File** tab, to switch from the Backstage view.

    g. Observe that a message appears below the Ribbon indicating that the Automatic replies are turned on.

    > It might take several minutes for the change to be evident.

Student 02

4. Test the Out of Office Assistant feature.

    a. Create an email message to your partner with the subject **Lunch** and the message **Want to meet at Phil's for lunch tomorrow?**

    b. Send the message.

    > A desktop alert briefly flashes on your screen informing you of your partner's status.

c. Observe that you received a new message from your partner.

d. Select the new message that you have received from your partner.

e. Observe that the **Automatic reply : Lunch** message appears in the subject line, indicating that the Automatic Replies feature is turned on.

> Student 02   Thu 11:42 AM
> Automatic reply: Lunch

---

5. **What happens when you send a message to someone who has turned on the Automatic Replies?**

   a) The message sits in your Outbox folder until the individual returns.

   b) The message is sent and you are alerted to the fact that the recipient is out of office.

   c) The message is returned to your Inbox folder.

   d) The message sits in your Drafts folder until the individual returns.

Student 01

6. Turn off the Out of Office Assistant feature.

   > Make sure that you complete this activity so that the Out Of Office Assistant does not continue sending automatic replies to your incoming messages.

   a. On the status bar, select the **Automatic Replies** option.

   b. In the **Automatic Replies** dialog box, select the **Do not send automatic replies** option to turn off the Out of Office feature.

   c. Click **OK** to close the **Automatic Replies** dialog box.

TOPIC E
Create a Contact Group

You have notified others that you are out of office. When addressing email messages, you may find that you are frequently sending messages to the same set of people. In this topic, you will create a contact group so that you can easily send messages to multiple users.

In your organization, you may need to frequently send email messages to groups of people. Every time you do this, you have to type or select multiple user names. You may miss some users, or you may send a message to someone who is not supposed to receive it. Using Outlook, you can create a contact group, with which you can quickly send an email message to multiple users.

Contact Groups

Definition:

A *contact group* is a collection of user names commonly referred to by one descriptive name. It is used to quickly address and send an email message to multiple users. Contact Groups are stored in the **Contacts** folder and are identified by their group names and the term **Group.**

Example:

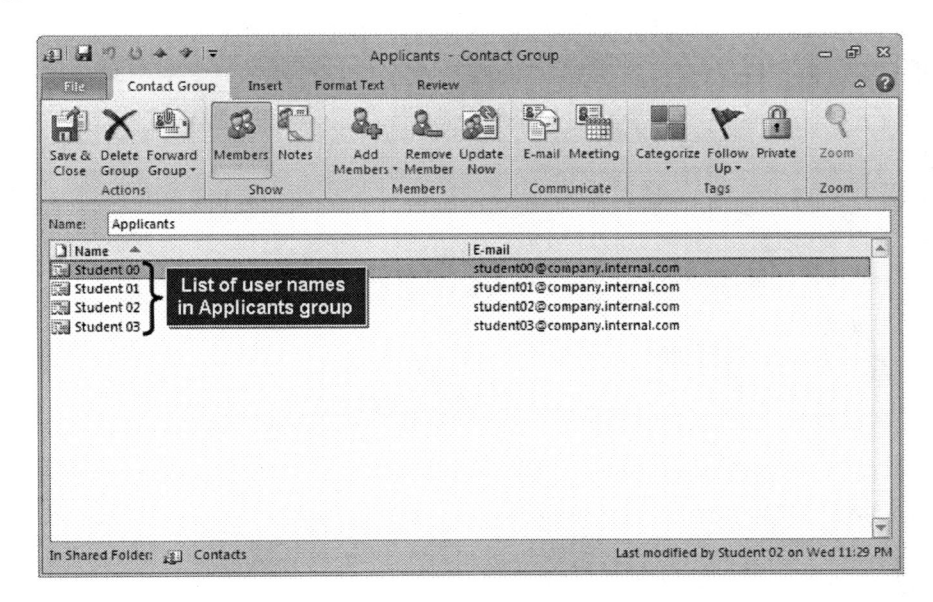

Figure 1-11: List of users in a contact group named Applicants.

The Contact group was previously referred to as the Distribution List.

The individual user names in a contact group can be contacts from the Outlook **Contacts** folder or names from the Address book. List names can include spaces and are not case-sensitive.

How to Create a Contact Group

Procedure Reference: Create a Contact Group

To create a contact group:

1. On the **Home** tab, in the **New** group, from the **New Items** drop-down list, choose **More Items→Contact Group.**
2. In the **Name** text box, type a name for the contact group.
3. On the **Contact Group** tab, in the **Members** group, click **Add Members** and choose the From Address Book option, to open the **Select Members: Global Address List** dialog box.
4. From the **Address Book** drop-down list, select the address book that contains the email addresses that you want to include in your contact group.
5. Add the names you want to include in this contact group.
   - In the **Search** text box, type the user name and then click **Members**.
   - In the **Name** list, double-click the user name, or;
   - In the **Name** list, click the user name and then click **Members**.
6. Click **OK** to display the user names in the **Contact Group** form.
7. On the **Contact Group** tab, in the **Actions** group, click **Save & Close** to create the contact group.

Procedure Reference: Modify a Contact Group Temporarily

To modify an existing contact group temporarily:

1. On the **Contact Group** tab, in the **Communicate** group, click **E-mail** to send an email to the group.
2. In the **To** text box of the email message address section, click the plus sign preceding the contact group name.
3. In the **Expand List** message box, click **OK** to replace the contact group with its members.
4. Add or delete the user name(s) from the **To** text box.

Procedure Reference: Modify a Contact Group Permanently

To modify an existing contact group permanently:

1. On the Quick launch bar, click **Contacts.**
2. In the **Contacts** folder, double-click the contact group that you wish to modify in order to open it.
3. Edit the names list as desired.
   - Choose **Add Members→From Outlook Contacts** to add additional names from the Contacts folder.
   - Choose **Add Members→From Address Book** to add additional names from the address book.
   - Choose **Add Members→New E-mail contact** to add a new contact.
   - To delete a name, select the name and click **Remove.**
4. On the **Contact Group** tab, in the **Actions** group, click **Save & Close** to update the list.

Procedure Reference: Print a Contact Group

To print a contact group:

1. On the Quick launch bar, click **Contacts.**
2. Open the contact group you want to print.
3. In the **Contact Group** form, select the **File** tab, and choose **Print.**
4. In the **Print** section, click the **Print** button.

Procedure Reference: Update Contact Group Member Information

To update contact group member information:

> You can update the contact group member information only on the Exchange server.

1. On the Outlook Exchange server, display the **Properties** dialog box of the contact group member whose information needs to be edited.
    a. Choose **Start→Programs→Microsoft Exchange Server 2010→Exchange Management Console.**
    b. In the **Exchange Management Console** window, click **Recipient Configuration** to expand it.
    c. Click **Mailbox** to display all the users in the right pane.
    d. Right-click the contact group member name whose contact information you want to update, and choose **Properties.**
2. In the [User name] **Properties** dialog box, select the desired tabs and update the necessary information.
3. Click **OK** to update the information and close the dialog box.

ACTIVITY 1-6
Creating a Contact Group

Scenario:
As a career counselor at Our Global Company, a job placement agency, one of your responsibilities is to keep applicants informed of new job openings. You have been sending this information to applicants individually, but as the agency has grown, so has the number of applicants. You want to now create a shortcut for quickly addressing an ever-growing set of email messages.

1. Create a new contact group called **Applicants.**

    a. On the **Home** tab, in the **New** group, from the **New Items** drop-down list, select **More Items→Contact Group.**

    b. In the **Name** text box, type **Applicants**

2. Add your partner and two other users to the list.

    a. On the **Contact Group** tab, in the **Members** group, choose the **Add Members→From Address Book** option.

    b. In the **Select Members: Global Address List** dialog box, in the **Name** list, select your partner and two other user names.

    c. Click **Members.**

    d. Verify that the names you have selected are displayed in the **Members** text box. Click **OK** to display the user names in the contact group form.

    e. On the **Contact Group** tab, in the **Actions** group, click **Save & Close** to create the contact group.

ACTIVITY 1-7
Modifying a Contact Group

Scenario:
You need to send an email reminding those on the "Applicants" contact group to check the recent job posting. While you are working on the email, you receive a note that one of the applicants has obtained a permanent position. Therefore, you need to remove his name from the contact group within the email, as well as from the contact group itself.

1. Address an email to the newly created "Applicants" contact group.

    a. Open a new message window.

    b. In the message heading, click **To** to open the **Select Names: Global Address List** dialog box.

    c. From the **Address Book** drop-down list, select **Contacts**.

    d. Verify that the **Applicants** contact group is selected and click **To**.

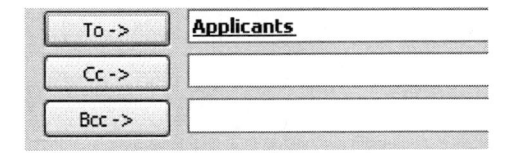

    e. Click **OK** to address the message.

2. **True or False? Within the To text box of the email message, Contact Groups are preceded by a plus sign icon.**

    ___ True
    ___ False

3. Within the email, edit the **Applicants** Contact Group to remove the last user name from the **To** text box.

    a. Click the plus sign preceding the **Applicants** contact group to expand the group.

    b. In the **Expand List** warning box, click **OK** to replace the contact group with its members.

    c. Select the last user name from the **To** text box and press **Delete**.

Lesson 1: Customizing Message Options 31

> You do not need to remove the semicolon preceding the user name.

4. Create and send an email.

   a. In the **Subject** text box, type *Reminder*

   b. In the message body, type *Be sure to check our website for new job postings.*

   c. Send the message.

5. Modify the "Applicants" contact group.

   a. On the Quick launch bar, select the **Contacts** folder.

   b. Open the **Applicants** contact group.

   c. From the **Name** list, select the last user name.

   d. On the **Contact Group** tab, in the **Members** group, click **Remove Member.**

   e. In the **Actions** group, click **Save & Close.**

INSTRUCTOR ACTIVITY 1-8
Updating Contact Group Member Information

Setup:
The Microsoft Exchange Server 2010 is configured.

Scenario:
One of the members in the contact group got promoted as a Consultant in your company. As the Exchange server administrator, you decide to update the contact information of that member.

1. On the Outlook Exchange server, display the **Properties** dialog box of one of the contact group members.

    a. On the server, choose **Start→All Programs→Microsoft Exchange Server 2010→ Exchange Management Console.**

    b. Expand **MS Exchange Out Premises**

    c. In the Exchange Management Console window, click **Recipient Configuration** to expand it.

    d. Click **Mailbox** to display all the users in the right pane.

    e. Right-click the contact group member name whose contact information you want to update, and choose **Properties.**

2. Update the contact group member information.

    a. In the [Student ##] **Properties** dialog box, select the **Organization** tab.

    b. In the **Title** text box, type *Consultant*

    c. In the **Company** text box, type *Our Global Company*

    d. Select the **Address & Phone** tab.

    e. In the **Phone numbers** section, in the **Business** text box, type the desired phone number.

    f. Click **OK** to update the information and close the dialog box.

TOPIC F
Insert a Hyperlink

You have created a contact group so that you can easily send email messages to multiple users. When sending messages, it is likely that at some point you may need to make reference to an Internet or intranet site in an email message. In this topic, you will insert a hyperlink into an email message so that the recipient can click the link and visit the website.

There might be instances where you are in a need to constantly refer clients and coworkers to various websites, both on the Internet and on your local intranet. You often refer to these sites in email messages that you create. Using Outlook, you can create a link to a specific site so that recipients can click the link to go directly to the referenced site.

Hyperlinks

Definition:
A *hyperlink* is an object, text, or a graphic that, when clicked, takes you to another location. Outlook allows you to create hyperlinks that can link to a web page, an email address, a network location, an Outlook location, or an Outlook item.

Example:

Here is the link that I promised to send Outlook:Inbox ← Outlook Inbox hyperlink

Thanks.

Here is the link to the website that we discussed.

http://www.ourglobalcompany.com ← URL hyperlink

Figure 1-12: Examples of a hyperlink.

Characteristics of Hyperlinks

Hyperlinks can be identified by:

- Text preceded by www or http://.
- Text underlined (though not always) and displayed in a different color (blue by default) than the rest of the text in the document.
- An object or an image surrounded by a border (though not always).
- The mouse pointer changing to a pointing hand when it moves over the hyperlink.

> When you type an address correctly, Outlook recognizes it as a hyperlink and converts it accordingly.

How to Insert a Hyperlink

Procedure Reference: Insert a Hyperlink in a Message

To insert a hyperlink in a message:

1. Within the email message, position your mouse pointer where you want to insert the hyperlink.
2. Create the hyperlink.
   - Type the hyperlink, or;
   - Create a hyperlink from the Internet Explorer window.
     a. Open the Internet Explorer window.
     b. Navigate to the website that you wish to add as a hyperlink.
     c. From the address bar, drag the address icon onto the message and then release the mouse button to add the link to the message.

> You can also create various hyperlinks in an open Outlook item by using the **Hyperlink** button in the **Links** group that is present on the **Insert** tab. The **Insert Hyperlink** dialog box allows you to set links to existing files or web pages, places within documents, or email addresses. See online help for assistance.

ACTIVITY 1-9
Inserting a Hyperlink in a Message

Scenario:
While you are out of office for the week, your assistant has agreed to take over your responsibilities. You need to send him an email message that provides him with the information necessary to access an important website, **http://www.ourglobalcompany.com**.

Student 01

1. Create a message that includes a link to the website.

    a. Display the **Inbox** folder.

    b. Address a new email message to your partner with the subject **Website** and the message *Here is a link to the website that we discussed.*

    c. Press **Enter** twice to add some space between the text body and the hyperlink.

    d. Type *http://www.ourglobalcompany.com* to create a hyperlink to the web page.

    e. Send the message.

Student 02

2. Open the **Website** message and test the link.

    a. Select the **Website** email message.

    b. In the **Reading** pane, click the link.

    > **Website**
    > Student 01
    > Sent: Wed 8/18/2010 10:29 PM
    > To: Student 02
    >
    > Here is the link to the website that we discussed.
    >
    > http://www.ourglobalcompany.com

    c. Observe that the site you have launched is displayed in the Internet Explorer window.

    d. Close the Internet Explorer window.

TOPIC G
Create Quick Steps

You have customized and managed your emails efficiently in Outlook. You may want to easily access the commands for frequently performed actions. In this topic, you will create quick steps.

Considering the volume of email messages sent and received, mail management features have become essential. Also, as email applications have become part of everyday communication, there are tasks that have become routine and mechanical. These tasks can be automated so that you do not need to use different commands to perform them each time. Outlook provides you with the Quick Steps feature, which has easy-to-use buttons that can perform multiple actions at once.

Quick Steps

Quick steps are commands that facilitate the performing of common tasks that involve multiple actions in a single-click. Quick steps make repetitive tasks easier and quicker. They are displayed in the **Quick Steps** group on the **Home** tab of the Ribbon. There are various default quick steps available for common tasks performed in Outlook and you can also create custom quick steps by using the **Create New** command, which displays the **Edit Quick Step** dialog box. You can also customize or delete quick steps by using the **Manage Quick Steps** dialog box.

Figure 1-13: The Quick Steps group displayed on the Home tab of the Ribbon.

Default Quick Steps
Some of the default quick steps include:
- **Move To:** Marks an email message as read and moves it to a specified folder.
- **Reply & Delete:** Allows you to reply to an email message and deletes the original message.
- **Done:** Marks an email message as read and moves it to a specified folder.
- **Team E-mail:** Used to forward an email message to the members of your team, as specified in the Global Address List.
- **To Manager:** Used to forward an email message to your manager, as specified in the Global Address List.

The Manage Quick Steps Dialog Box

The **Manage Quick Steps** dialog box allows you to customize or delete the existing quick steps. You can also add shortcut keys, add new quick steps, and display tooltips for a quick step.

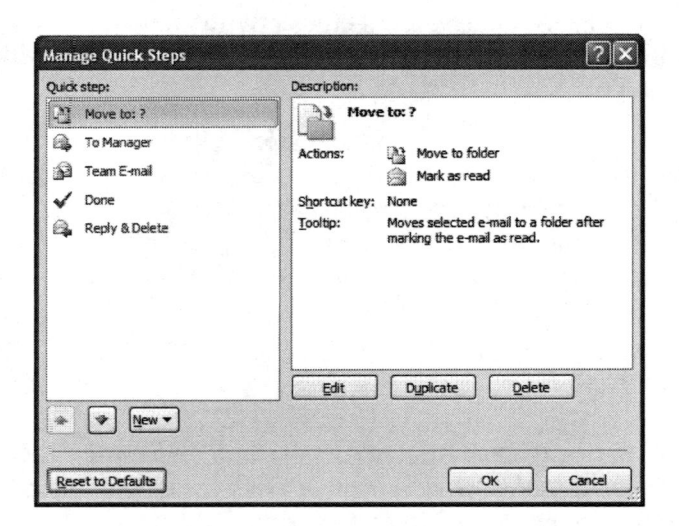

Figure 1-14: The components of the Manage Quick Steps dialog box.

There are several different components in the **Manage Quick Steps** dialog box.

Component	Description
Quick step list box	Displays the default quick steps such as **Move to, To Manager, Team E-mail, Done, Reply & Delete,** and **Create New** and any custom quick steps that you create.
Description section	Displays a description including the **Actions, Shortcut key,** and **Tooltip** for a selected quick step.
Up and down arrow buttons	Allow you to reorder quick steps in the **Quick step** list box and in the **Quick Steps** group on the **Home** tab.
New drop-down list	Displays options to add a new quick step.
Edit button	Allows you to edit a quick step.
Duplicate button	Allows you to duplicate a quick step.
Delete button	Allows you to delete a quick step.
Reset to Defaults	Allows you to reset to the default settings.

How to Create a Quick Step

Procedure Reference: Create a Quick Step

To create a quick step:

1. If necessary, switch to the Mail view.
2. In the Mail view, on the Ribbon, select the **Home** tab, and in the **Quick Steps** group, click **Create New.**
3. In the **Edit Quick Step** dialog box, in the **Actions** section, select the actions for the quick step.
   - From the **Choose an Action** drop-down list, select an action.
   - If necessary, click **Add Action,** and from the **Choose an Action** drop-down list, select an additional action to be added.
4. In the **Name** text box, enter a name for the new quick step.
5. If necessary, to left of the **Name** text box, click the icon, and in the **Choose an icon** dialog box, select an icon and click **OK** to change the icon for the new quick step.

ACTIVITY 1-10
Creating a Quick Step for Flagging an Email Message

Scenario:
You just sent an email message with a product list to your client. You might often want to flag this message for following up on them in future. Therefore, it will be helpful if you create a shortcut for sending these messages to this specific client.

1. Create a quick step for flagging an email message.

    a. On the **Home** tab, in the **Quick Steps** group, click **Create New** to display the **Edit Quick Step** dialog box.

    b. In the **Edit Quick Step** dialog box, in the **Name** text box, type *Flag Message* and to the left of the text box, click the **Click here to change the icon for this quick step** button to change the icon for the quick step.

    c. In the **Choose an icon** drop-down list, in the third row, select the third icon and click **OK** to add it as the icon for the quick step.

    d. In the **Edit Quick Step** dialog box, in the **Actions** section, from the **Choose an Action** drop-down list, in the **Categories, Tasks and Flags** section, select **Flag Message.**

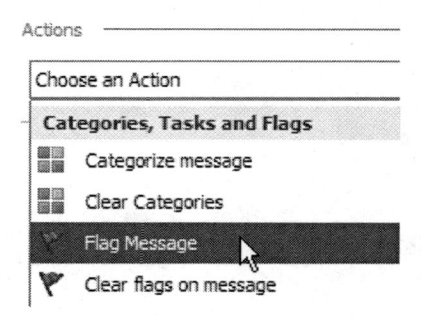

    e. From the **Choose flag** drop-down list, select **Next Week** to add an action to the quick step.

    f. In the **Optional** section, in the **Tooltip text** text box, click and type *Flag an email message for follow-up next week.*

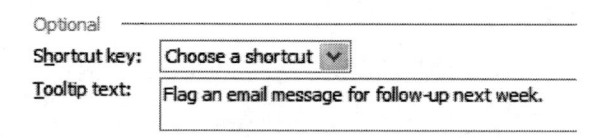

    g. Click **Finish** to add the quick step.

---

40   Lesson 1: Customizing Message Options

h. On the **Home** tab, in the **Quick Steps** group, observe that the **Flag Message** quick step has been created and is displayed.

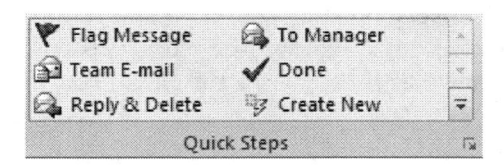

2. Flag an existing email message.

   a. Display the **Sent Items** folder.

   b. Select the **Performance Appraisal** message.

   c. On the **Home** tab, in the **Quick Steps** group, click **Flag Message** to flag the message.

Lesson 1 Follow-up

In this lesson, you modified message settings, delivery options, and the message format; notified others when you were out of office; created a contact group; inserted hyperlinks; and created quick steps. This experience and knowledge enables you to customize your messages, to suit your requirement.

1. **Which message importance and sensitivity levels are you likely to use?**

2. **What are the delivery options you are likely to use and why?**

2 Organizing and Locating Messages

Lesson Time: 1 hour(s), 30 minutes

Lesson Objectives:

In this lesson, you will organize and locate Outlook messages.

You will:

- Sort messages using multiple criteria.
- Find items that contain specific text.
- Find Outlook items based on multiple search criteria.
- Apply a filter to messages.
- Organize messages.
- Set junk email options.

Introduction

You customized email messages by setting the various message options, and you have used basic methods for organizing Outlook messages and other items. However, there are alternate methods to organize Outlook messages that you may find even more effective. In this lesson, you will use more advanced features to search for Outlook messages and display them.

In any organization, there is always a need to refer to old email messages while resolving an issue or making a decision. A large collection of messages can make it difficult to quickly locate the ones that you need. In addition, you may not remember the subject or the message text. This would make it a tedious, and perhaps even futile job, and your search would be in vain. Outlook provides advanced features that can minimize your search effort, and help you to locate specific messages quickly.

TOPIC A
Sort Messages Using Multiple Criteria

As an experienced Outlook user, you have most likely used the simplest method of sorting messages—clicking a column header to arrange messages by that column. You may now want to fine-tune that sort order using more than one column at a time. In this topic, you will sort Outlook items using multiple criteria.

Sorting a long list of items can help you to quickly locate a specific item. However, sorting by only one column might not give you the results that you are looking for. Using Outlook, you can sort by a second, third, or fourth column, making it even easier to locate items in a long list.

Sort Criteria

Definition:

Sort criteria are categories by which a list of Outlook items can be sorted. Criteria are usually specified by a field and a sort order.

Example:

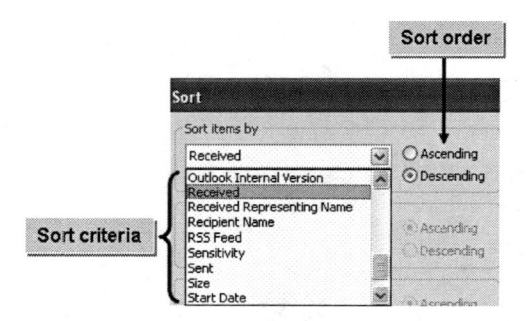

Figure 2-1: Sort criteria options for Inbox messages.

Types of Sorts

While a simple sort arranges the items in an order specified by one field and a sorting order, a multiple-criteria sort arranges items based on more than one field. Examples of how you might sort an Inbox include:

Sort Type	Example
Simple sort	Sort by sender.
Two criteria sort	Sort by sender, then by date received.
Three criteria sort	Sort by sender, then by date received, then by subject.

How to Sort Messages Using Multiple Criteria

Procedure Reference: Sort Messages Using Multiple Criteria

To sort messages using multiple criteria:

1. Display the folder containing the messages you want to sort.
2. On the **View** tab, in the **Current View** group, click **View Settings.**
3. In the **Advanced View Settings : Compact** dialog box, click the **Sort** option.
4. In the **Sort** dialog box, from the **Sort items by** drop-down list, select the field to sort by.

> If the field you want is not in the **Sort items by** drop-down list, you can use the **Select available fields from** drop-down list to select additional fields.

5. Select either the **Ascending** or **Descending** sort option.
6. From the **Then by** drop-down list, select the second field to sort by.
7. Select either the **Ascending** or **Descending** sort option.
8. If you need additional sort criteria, repeat steps 6 and 7.
9. Click **OK** to close the **Sort** dialog box.
10. Click **OK** to close the **Advanced View Settings : Compact** dialog box and perform the sort.

ACTIVITY 2-1
Sorting Messages Using Multiple Criteria

Scenario:
You are preparing a presentation for a client and want to review the correspondence you have received from him in the past few months. Rather than searching through your long list of email messages, you want to display all messages from this contact in order by the date they were received.

1. Sort the Inbox by name/sender and then by the date the messages were received.

    a. Display the Inbox folder.

    b. On the **View** tab, in the **Current View** group, click **View Settings.**

    c. In the **Advanced View Settings : Compact** dialog box, click the **Sort** option.

    d. In the **Sort** dialog box, from the **Sort items by** drop-down list, scroll up and select **From.**

    e. If necessary, next to the **Sort items by** drop-down list, select the **Ascending** sort option.

f. From the **Then by** drop-down list, scroll down and select **Received** to sort the Inbox messages by the date they were received.

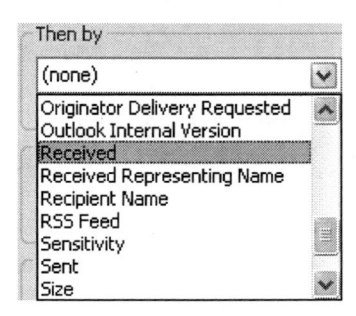

> Be sure you selected **Received** from the **Then by** drop-down list (the second drop-down list from the top), not from the **Sort items by** drop-down list.

g. If necessary, next to the **Then by** drop-down list box, select the **Ascending** sort option.

h. Click **OK** to close the **Sort** dialog box.

i. If necessary, in the **Microsoft Outlook** warning dialog boxes that appear, click **Yes**.

j. Observe that in the **Advanced View Settings : Compact** dialog box, next to the **Sort** option, the conditions that are set, are displayed.

k. Click **OK** to close the **Advanced View Settings : Compact** dialog box.

2. **True or False? Messages are listed in alphabetical or numerical order by senders' user names. For each sender, messages are listed in the order they were received, with the newest messages listed at the top.**

___ True

___ False

TOPIC B
Find Messages Using Instant Search

You have sorted and rearranged all the items in your Inbox. Even after sorting, you may find it difficult to search for a specific message from a huge set of messages. In this topic, you will find messages that contain specific text.

When it comes to email messages, most of us tend to keep more messages than are necessary, for fear we might need them again. This practice can result in one or more folders with hundreds of messages. Using Outlook's Instant Search feature makes locating items that contain specific text quicker and easier, despite the number of messages we have stored.

Instant Search

Instant Search is a feature that allows you to search email messages and other tasks in Outlook. There are also options that allow you to widen the search criteria. The Instant Search pane is available in the **Mail, Calendar, Contacts, Tasks, Notes, Folder List,** and **Journal** folders.

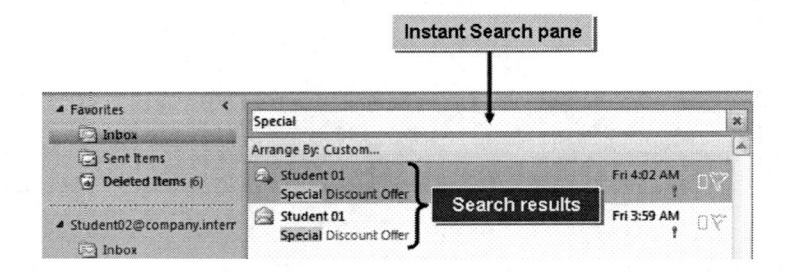

Figure 2-2: The Instant Search pane in the Inbox.

The Search Tools Contextual Tab

The **Search Tools** Contextual tab is displayed when you click or type in the Instant Search text box. It supports various options displayed in many groups.

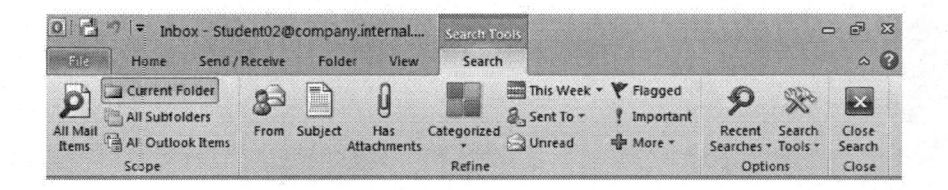

Figure 2-3: The Search Tools Contextual tab provides various search options.

Search Tools Contextual Tab Group	Description
Scope	Provides options to specify the scope of the search, such as whether it is restricted to a specific folder, specific subfolders, or all views in Outlook.
Refine	Provides options to refine the search by specifying advanced search options using specific search criteria, such as from a particular sender, with a particular subject, whether it has attachments, when the message was sent or received, or whether it is unread.
Options	Provides recent searches along with other search tools that you can use. You can display the **Advanced Find** dialog box, and also modify the search options, by using the **Outlook Options** dialog box.
Close	Allows you to terminate the current search and hide the **Search Tools** contextual tab.

The Search Tab

The **Search** tab is located in the **Outlook Options** dialog box. It has two sections: The **Sources** and the **Results** pane.

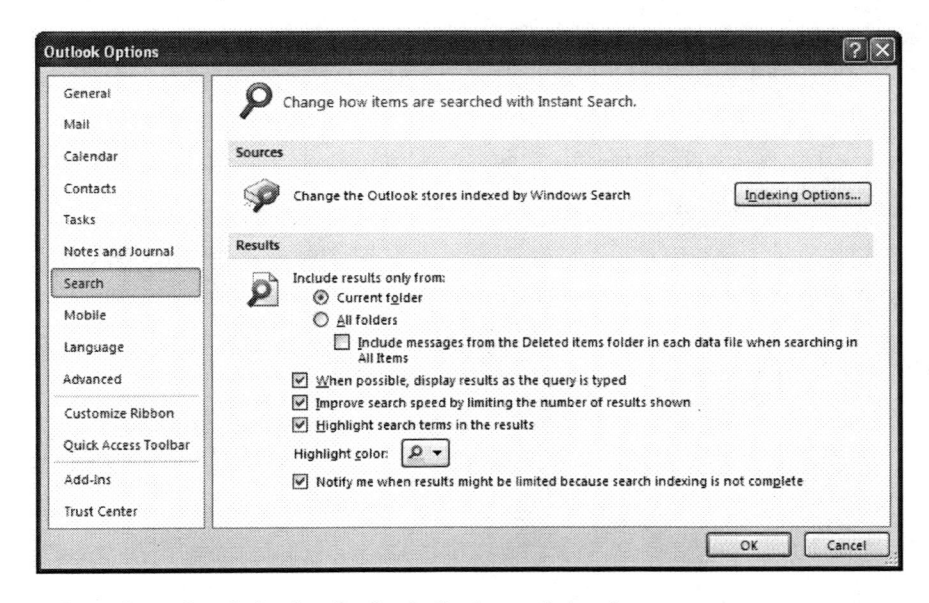

Figure 2-4: The Search tab in the Outlook Options dialog box.

Section	Description
Sources	Changes the way Outlook stores messages indexed by Window Search.
Results	Allows you to customize the way you want your result to be shown. It includes results from the Current folder and All folders. You can also improve your search result by limiting the number of results shown.

How to Find Messages Using Instant Search

Procedure Reference: Search for Items in Outlook Using Instant Search

To search for items in Outlook using Instant Search:

1. Select the folders that are to be searched.
2. In the **Instant Search** text box, enter the search text.

> The items of the selected folder that contain the search text are displayed in the **Instant Search Results** pane, with the search text highlighted.

3. On the **Search Tools** contextual tab, in the **Scope** group, set the desired option to specify criteria for the search.
   - Click **All Mail Items** to search the mail items in all folders.
   - Click **Current Folder** to search within the current folder.
   - Click **All Outlook Items** to search all items.
4. On the **Search Tools** contextual tab, in the **Refine** group, set an option.
   - Click **From** and in the **Instant Search** text box, specify the criteria to search for messages from a particular sender.
   - Click **Subject** and in the **Instant Search** text box, specify the criteria to search for messages with a particular subject.
   - Click **Has Attachments** to search for messages that contain attachments.
   - From the **Categorized** drop-down list, select an option to search by category.
     - Select **Any Category** to search for messages from any category.
     - Select **No Categories** to search for messages that are not categorized.
   - From the **This Week** drop-down list, select an option to search for messages by date.
   - From the **Sent To** drop-down list, select an option to search for messages by recipients.
     - Select **Sent To: Me** to search for messages that were sent directly to you.
     - Select **CC: Me** to search for messages in which you were on the CC list.
     - Select **Not Sent Directly to Me** to search for messages that were not sent directly to you.
     - Select **Sent to Another Recipient** to search for messages that were sent to another recipient.
   - Click **Unread** to display unread messages that match the search criteria.
   - Click **Flagged** to display flagged messages that match the search criteria.
   - Click **Important** to display messages that have a specific priority level and match the search criteria.
   - From the **More** drop-down list, select an option to display messages with the chosen field, and that match the search criteria.
5. On the **Search Tools** contextual tab, in the **Options** group, set the required option.
   - From the **Recent Searches** drop-down list, select a recent search to repeat the search.
   - From the **Search Tools** drop-down list, select an option to use advanced search tools.

- Click **Indexing Status** to check the number of items that need to be indexed.
- Click **Locations to Search** and choose an email account, to perform a search in the account.
- Click **Advanced Find** to perform a search by using advanced search criteria.
- Click **Search Options** to specify or modify the search options in the **Outlook Options** dialog box.

6. If necessary, in the **Close** group of the **Search Tools** contextual tab, click **Close Search** to close the current search.

ACTIVITY 2-2
Finding a Message Containing Specific Text

Scenario:
You need to find an email that you received from a member of your team several weeks ago. You do not want to spend too much time searching through your Inbox to locate this message; you want to find it quickly.

1. Find all messages in the **Inbox** folder that contain the text "Job."

    a. In the View pane, in the Instant Search text box, type **Job**

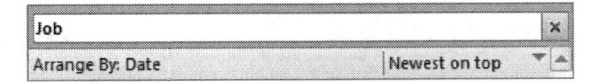

    b. Observe that, from the **Inbox** folder, a message containing the text that you typed in, is displayed in the **Instant Search Results** pane with the search text highlighted.

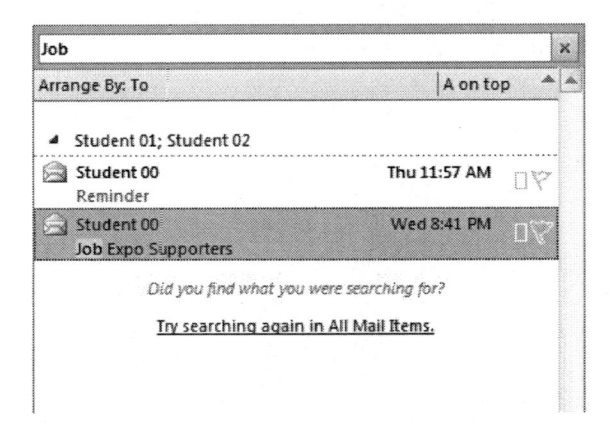

2. Search all email folders at once.

    a. On the **Search Tools** contextual tab, in the **Scope** group, select **All Mail Items** to search all email folders at once.

    > It might take several minutes for the change to be evident.

b. Observe that all the messages that contain the term **Job** are displayed in the **All Mail Items** folder list.

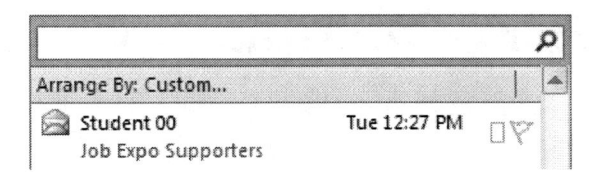

c. On the **Search text** contextual tool tab, in the **Close** group, click **Close Search.**

TOPIC C
Find Messages Using Multiple Criteria

You performed a quick search of messages that contain specific text using the Instant Search feature. In addition to finding items that contain specific text, you may also want to locate messages that meet multiple criteria. In this topic, you will find Outlook messages based on multiple criteria.

Perhaps you need to locate an item that not only contains certain specific words, but also need to search for messages using various criteria based on your requirement. Outlook's Advanced Find Feature allows you to quickly find items that meet multiple criteria.

The Query Builder Feature

The *Query Builder* feature narrows your search by providing multiple search fields. In the **Define more criteria** section, the **Field** drop-down list displays more search fields in the Query Builder, and you can select the search fields from the list. You can also apply different conditions and values. The **Logical Group** allows you to check for logical conditions within the specified criteria and you can use the logical **AND** or **OR** operator to develop the query and move clauses up or down.

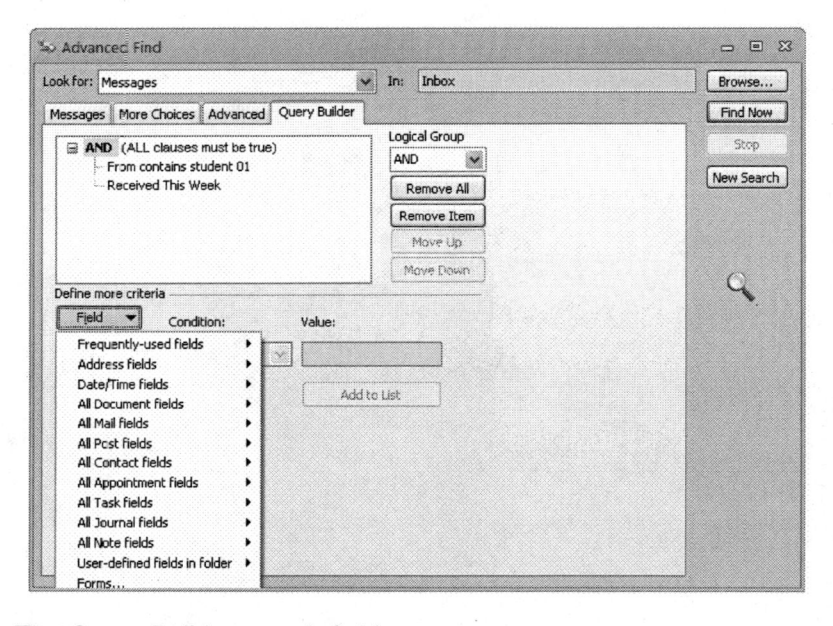

Figure 2-5: The Query Builder search fields.

The Advanced Find Dialog Box

The **Advanced Find** dialog box is used to locate items that meet multiple levels of criteria that can be based on almost any field in any Outlook folder. The found items are displayed at the bottom of the dialog box rather than in the Outlook folder contents list. This is a contextual feature, and the default tab that is displayed depends upon the current items in Outlook.

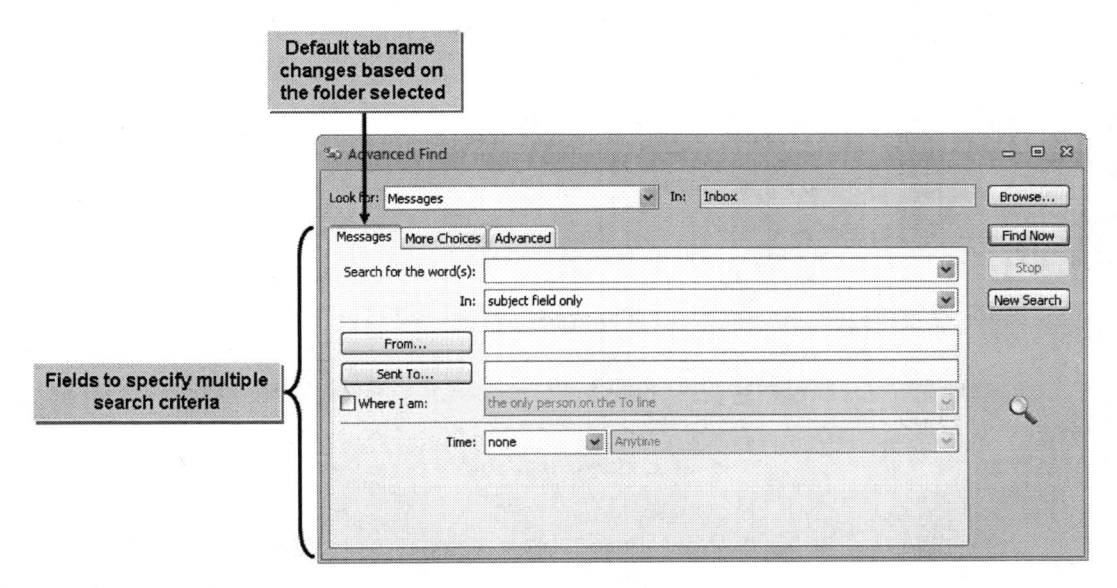

Figure 2-6: The options in the Advanced Find dialog box.

There are several options in the **Advanced Find** dialog box to help you locate items.

Option	Allows You To
Look for drop-down list.	Select the types of Outlook items to search for, such as messages, tasks, notes, appointments, meetings, and contacts.
Browse button	Specify the folder in which the search needs to be performed.
Default tab	Enter the details of the selected item, depending upon the current item that is selected. The options displayed on this tab depend on the choice that is made in the **Look for** text box.
More Choices tab	Categorize email messages based on the read or unread status, the presence of attachments, the priority level, color categories, the flagged status, and size.
Advanced tab	Define criteria based on different fields or conditions, or on specific values.
Find Now button	Look for the particular word or phrase that is specified in the **Search for the word(s)** text box.
New Search button	Clear the current search and perform a new search.

How to Find Messages Using Multiple Criteria

Procedure Reference: Find Messages Using Multiple Criteria

To find messages using multiple criteria:

1. On the **Search Tools** contextual tab, in the **Options** group, from the **Search Tools** drop-down list, select **Advanced Find.**
2. In the **Advanced Find** dialog box, from the **Look for** drop-down list, select the messages that you want to search for.
3. In the **Search for the word(s)** text box, type the search text.
4. If necessary, click **Browse,** and in the **Select Folder(s)** dialog box, select the folder in which to search, and click **OK** to display the appropriate folder in the **In** text box.
5. If necessary, in the **From** text box, specify a person's name whose email you need to search for.
6. Click **Find Now** to display the items that match the criteria in the **Advanced Find** dialog box.
7. If necessary, in the **Advanced Find** dialog box, select the **More Choices** tab and choose the required options.
    - From the **Color Categories** drop-down list, select a color category to filter the search results by.
    - Check the **Only items that are** check box to search for read or unread messages.
    - Check the **Only items with** check box to search for messages with attachments.
    - Check the **Whose importance is** check box to search for messages with a normal, low, or high priority.
    - Check the **Only items which** check box to search for messages that are flagged or completed.
    - From the **Size** drop-down list, select the desired option, and in the text box, enter the size to search for messages of the specified size.
8. If necessary, select the **Advanced** tab and specify the desired options.
    a. In the **Define more criteria** section, from the **Field** drop-down list, select a particular field and specify the conditions and values.
    b. Click **Add to List** to add the criteria to the **Find items that match this criteria** list box.
9. If necessary, click **Find Now** to search with the specified criteria.

Procedure Reference: Find Items Using Query Builder

To search for items using Query Builder:

1. Display the folder you want to search.
2. On the **Search Tools** contextual tab, in the **Options** group, from the **Search Tools** drop-down list, select **Advanced Find.**
3. In the **Advanced Find** dialog box, select the **Query Builder** tab.
4. From the **Look for** drop-down list, select the item that you want to search for.
5. In the **Define more criteria** section, from the **Field** drop-down list, select the field in which the items are to be searched.
6. In the **Condition** drop-down list, select the required condition for the selected field.
7. In the **Value** text box, enter the value to be searched.

8. Click **Add to List** to add the criteria, which is then displayed in the dialog box.
9. Click **Find Now** to display the search results.
10. Repeat steps (5), (6), (7), and (8) for additional search criteria.

> You can also delete search fields in Query Builder by clicking **Remove** in the list of search fields.

ACTIVITY 2-3
Finding Messages Using Multiple Criteria

Scenario:
You asked a potential job candidate to send you her resume, with high importance assigned to the message. After a long break, you are back at the office and now need to quickly find all email messages that contain the word "resume" and are marked high importance.

1. Set up the search to find messages containing the keyword **resume**.

    a. Click the Instant Search text box to display the **Search Tools** contextual tab.

    b. On the **Search Tools** contextual tab, in the **Options** group, from the **Search Tools** drop-down list, select **Advanced Find**.

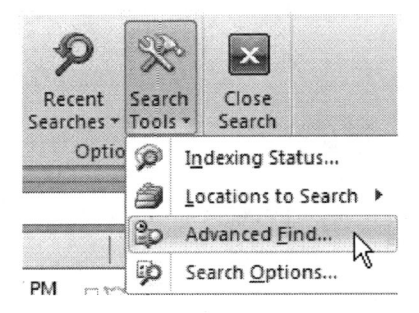

    c. In the **Advanced Find** dialog box, from the **Look for** drop-down list, verify that **Messages** is selected.

    d. In the **Search for the word(s)** text box, type *resume*

    e. From the **In** drop-down list, select **subject field and message body**.

2. Narrow the search to messages that have been assigned a high importance level.

    a. In the **Advanced Find** dialog box, select the **More Choices** tab.

    b. Check the **Whose importance is** check box.

c. From the **Whose importance is** drop-down list, select **high**.

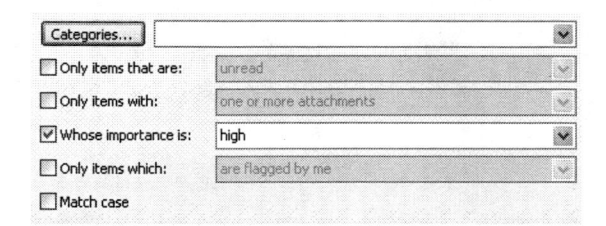

d. Click **Find Now** to find the messages.

3. True or False? Items that contain the word "resume" and have a high importance level are displayed at the bottom of the Advanced Find window.

    ___ True

    ___ False

4. Open the message and then return to **Inbox** folder list view.

    a. From the **Messages: Containing resume - Advanced Find** window, double-click the **Samantha Alvarez Resume.htm** message.

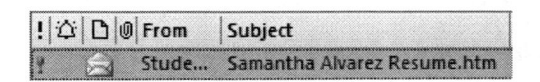

    b. Close the Message window.

    c. Close the **Messages: Containing resume - Advanced Find** window.

ACTIVITY 2-4
Finding Messages Using Query Builder

Setup:
The **Inbox** folder is displayed.

Scenario:
Since one of your team members is going on vacation, you have decided to allocate an uncompleted project task to another team member. In order to keep that team member updated on the project status, you decide to provide him with all of the email that contains the project details that you have received during this week. Rather than searching through your long list of email messages, you want to display all messages that you have received from this contact during this week.

1. Set up the search to find messages from a specific user.

    a. On the **Search Tools** contextual tab, in the **Options** group, from the **Search Tools** drop-down list, select **Advanced Find.**

    b. In the **Advanced Find** dialog box, select the **Query Builder** tab.

    c. From the **Look for** drop-down list, verify that **Messages** is selected.

    d. In the **Define more criteria** section, from the **Field** drop-down list, select **All Mail fields→From.**

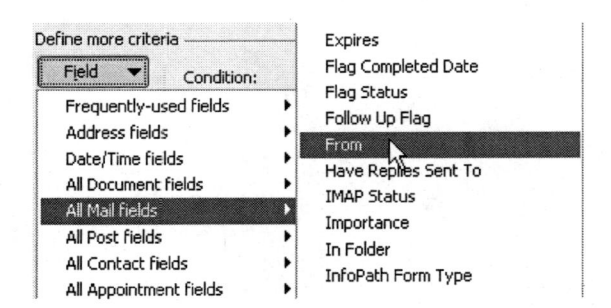

    e. From the **Condition** drop-down list, verify that the **contains** option is selected.

    f. In the **Value** text box, enter the name of your partner to display all the messages received from that partner.

    g. Click **Add to List** to add the criteria, to the list displayed in the dialog box.

2. Add an additional criteria to display the emails sent from that user during the past one week only.

a. In the **Define more criteria** section, from the **Field** drop-down list, select **Date/Time fields→Received.**

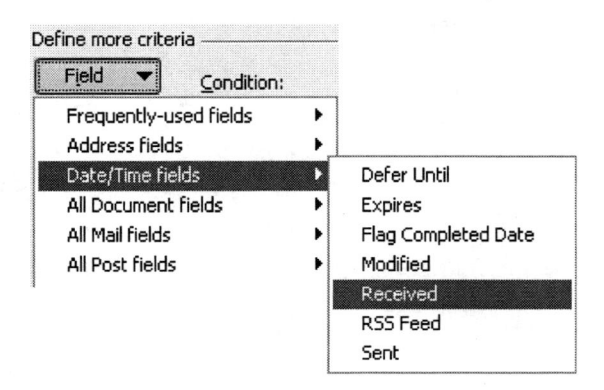

```
Define more criteria
 Field  ▼  Condition:
  Frequently-used fields  ▶
  Address fields          ▶
  Date/Time fields        ▶   Defer Until
  All Document fields     ▶   Expires
  All Mail fields         ▶   Flag Completed Date
  All Post fields         ▶   Modified
                              Received
                              RSS Feed
                              Sent
```

b. From the **Condition** drop-down list, choose **This Week.**

c. Click **Add to List** to add the criteria, to the list displayed in the dialog box.

d. Click **Find Now** to display the search results.

e. Observe that all the messages from your specified partner that were received during this week are displayed in the dialog box.

f. Close the **Message: Advanced-Advanced Find** dialog box.

TOPIC D
Filter Messages

You have located all the Outlook items using advanced Outlook search features. When you have numerous messages in your Inbox, you may want to display only those messages sent from a specific individual and filter the rest of the emails. In this topic, you will use Outlook to display only those messages that are of interest to you.

You know you will get around to cleaning up your Inbox one of these days, and you are finding it very distracting to have all of those messages that you have already read, displayed. It would help you focus if you had a "fresh start" each morning, with just that day's messages being displayed in the Inbox. Using an Outlook filter allows you to control exactly what is displayed in a folder.

Filters

A *filter* is a set of criteria you can apply to a folder to display only those items that meet specified conditions. Filters are specific to the selected folder and cannot be applied to another folder. When a filter criteria is applied to a folder, the condition that is specified is displayed next to the **Filter** button in the **Advanced View Settings** dialog box. The filtered view of a folder remains the same until the set of criteria specified is removed.

> Unlike sorting, which displays all items but in a different order, a filter displays only those items that meet the specified criteria.

Uses of Filters

Filtering may be useful in situations where you want to view certain items within a folder that meet specific conditions such as:

- Messages pertaining to only one project.
- Messages from one user.
- Only items that are unread.
- Today's messages only.
- All messages you sent to one person prior to a specified date.

The Filter Dialog Box

The **Filter** dialog box offers a variety of tabs with options that you can use to select and organize your filter criteria.

Figure 2-7: The Filter dialog box with filter criteria specified.

Tab	Description
Default tab	Filter items based on certain criteria such as selected search words, the subject field frequently used, text fields, or time. The options displayed on this tab depend on the folder selected.
More Choices	Filters items based on the read/unread status, attachments, priority level, color categories, flagged status, and actual size of the email.
Advanced	Filters items using additional or custom fields.
SQL	Filters items that match the criteria you type. It duplicates the filter you set on the **More Choices** tab. Other tabs will be unavailable if the **SQL** tab is selected.

How to Filter Messages

Procedure Reference: Filter Messages

To filter messages:

1. Display the folder containing the messages you want to filter.
2. From the **View** tab, in the **Current View** group, click **View Settings.**
3. In the **Advanced View Settings :** [Folder name] dialog box, click **Filter.**
4. Use the **More Choices, Advanced,** or **SQL** tab to choose or set filter options.

> The first tab that is related to the selected folder will, by default, be one of the three named tabs (More Choices, Advanced, SQL) intended for choosing or setting filter options.

5. Click **OK** to close the **Filter** dialog box.
6. In the **Microsoft Office Outlook** warning box, click **Yes** to apply the filter.

> Information about the filter you applied is displayed to the right of the **Filter** button.

7. Click **OK** to close the **Advanced View Settings :** [Folder name] dialog box and apply the filter.

> Similarly, you can filter other Outlook items such as contacts, tasks, and sand journals.

Procedure Reference: Clear a Filter

To clear a filter:

1. Display the contents of the folder that has the filter you want to clear.
2. Display the **Advanced View Settings** dialog box.
3. In the **Advanced View Settings** dialog box, click **Filter** to open the **Filter** dialog box.
4. Click **Clear All** to clear the filter.
5. Click **OK,** as necessary, to close any open dialog boxes.

Microsoft® Office Outlook® 2010: Level 2

ACTIVITY 2-5
Filtering Messages

Setup:
The Inbox is displayed.

Scenario:
You need to refer to a message that you sent earlier today to verify a due date. Since you have many messages in your Sent Items folder, you want to display only those messages sent to a specific individual. You remember that you also used the Copy address field to copy in another user name. However, after the due date, you realize that you do not need to refer to the messages sent to the individual anymore.

1. Set the filter for the messages in your **Sent Items** folder to display only those sent to a specific user.

   a. Select the **Sent Items** folder.

   b. On the **View** tab, in the **Current View** group, click **View Settings**.

   c. In the **Advanced View Settings: Sent To** dialog box, click **Filter**.

   d. In the **Filter** dialog box, on the **Messages** tab, click **Sent To**.

   e. In the **Select Names: Global Address List** dialog box, from the **Name** list, select **Student 00**.

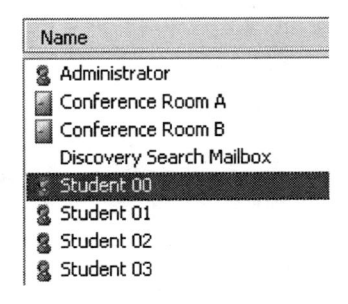

   ```
   Name
   • Administrator
   • Conference Room A
   • Conference Room B
     Discovery Search Mailbox
   • Student 00
   • Student 01
   • Student 02
   • Student 03
   ```

   f. At the bottom of the dialog box, click **Sent To**.

   ```
   Sent To ->  | Student 00
   ```

   g. Click **OK** to close the **Select Names: Global Address List** dialog box.

2. Set the filter for the messages in your **Sent Items** folder to display those messages that contain an entry of your partner in the **Cc** address field.

   a. In the **Filter** dialog box, select the **Advanced** tab.

Lesson 2: Organizing and Locating Messages   65

b. In the **Define more criteria** section, from the **Field** drop-down list, select **Address fields→Cc**.

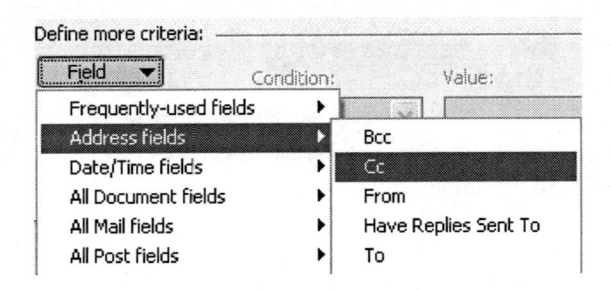

c. In the **Value** text box, type your partner's name.

d. Click **OK** to close the **Filter** dialog box.

e. In the **Microsoft Outlook** warning box, click **Yes** to add the criteria.

f. Information about the filter you applied is displayed to the right of the **Filter** button. Click **OK** to apply the filter and close the **Advanced View Settings** dialog box.

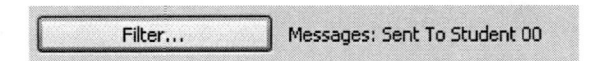

3. **True or False? Messages that satisfy the specified criteria are displayed in the Sent Items folder list.**

   ___ True

   ___ False

4. Remove the filter.

   a. On the **View** tab, in the **Current View** group, click **View Settings**.

   b. In the **Advanced View Settings: Sent to** dialog box, click **Filter**.

   c. In the **Filter** dialog box, click **Clear All** and then click **OK**.

   d. Observe that the filter option is turned **Off** and click **OK** to apply the changes.

TOPIC E
Organize Messages

You are now familiar with setting filters for email messages and other Outlook items. As your Inbox size increases, you may want to try to organize Outlook messages using various conditions. In this topic, you will use color, views, and rules to organize the messages in your Inbox.

With all of the sorting and finding methods you have used so far, you still had to read the message subject or sender information to identify messages you were interested in. It would be easier to identify specific messages, for example, if they appeared in red or green in your Inbox. Outlook allows you to identify and organize your messages in various ways.

The Arrangement Group

The *Arrangement group* displays your emails in your view preference. You can access the **Arrangement** group from the **View** tab. It is used to arrange emails by various categories.

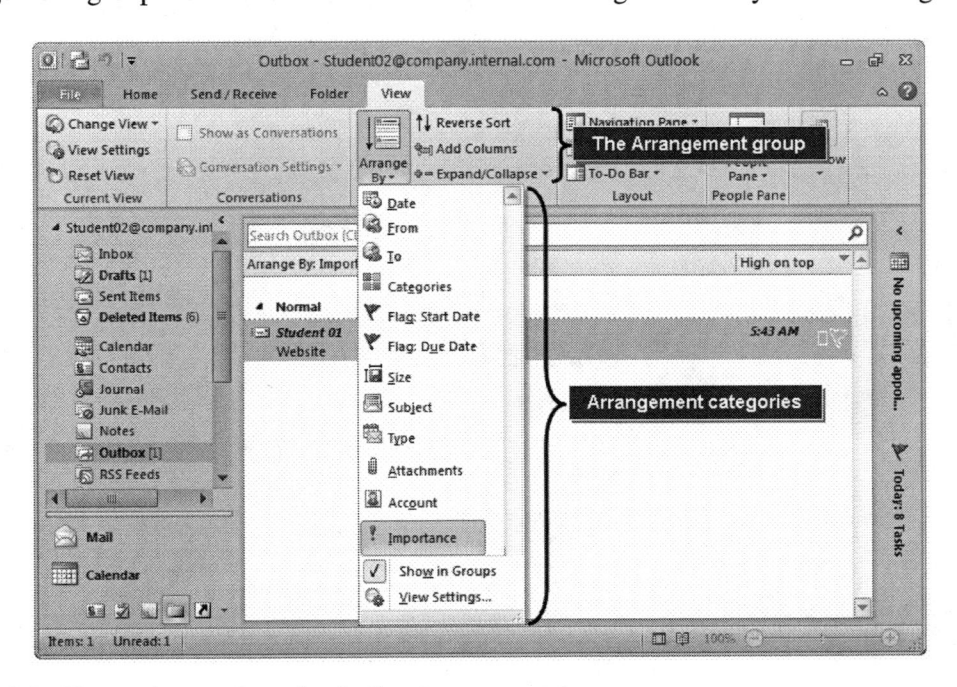

Figure 2-8: The various categories in the Arrangement group.

Category	Organizes Messages Based On
Date	The date and time of delivery.
From	The sender's name.
To	The receiver's name.
Categories	The various color categories.
Flag: Start Date	The start date. This is applied only for flagged messages.

Category	Organizes Messages Based On
Flag: Due Date	The due date. This is applied only for flagged messages.
Size	The size of the message.
Subject	The subject of the message.
Type	The types of messages.
Attachments	The attachments to messages.
Account	The users belonging to the same server account.
Importance	The various importance levels.

Conditional Formatting

Conditional Formatting enables you to change the appearance of Outlook items with Conditional Formatting rules. This is accomplished using the **Conditional Formatting** dialog box and it is accessed from the **View** tab using the **Advanced View Settings** dialog box. The **Conditional Formatting** dialog box contains default rules, and each rule has default font sizes and colors. For example, the default font size and color for the rule **Unread Messages** is **8 pt. Segoe UI**. You can also create your own rules and set your own fonts and conditions.

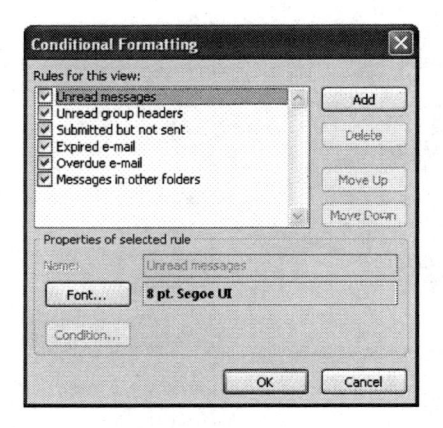

Figure 2-9: The Conditional Formatting dialog box.

The Rules Wizard

The *Rules Wizard* takes you step-by-step through the process of creating a rule. Rules created with the **Rules Wizard** contain a condition and an action, and they may also contain an exception.

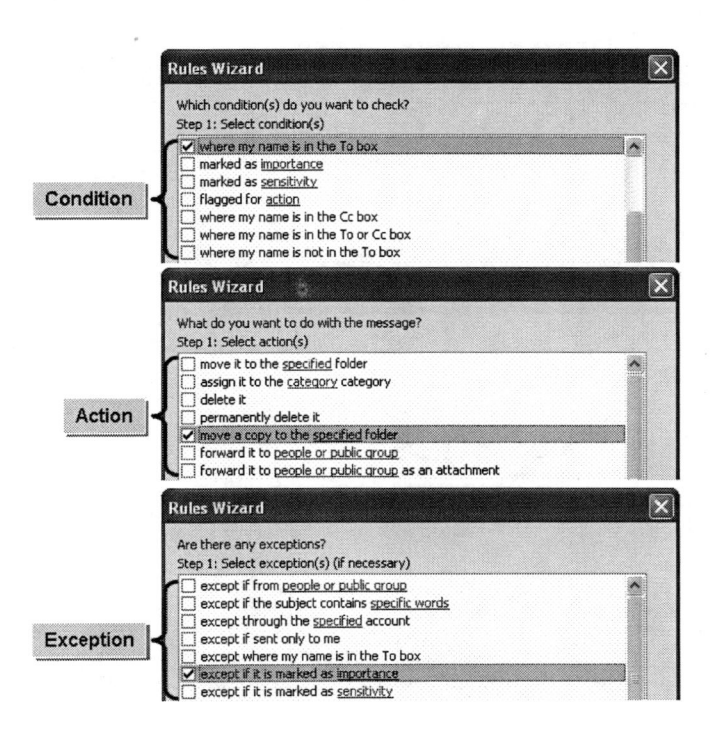

Figure 2-10: Rules with conditions, actions, and exceptions.

The **Rules Wizard** provides you with an assortment of rule templates—predefined rules that can be used as the basis for creating your own rules. These rules are located in three different template sections.

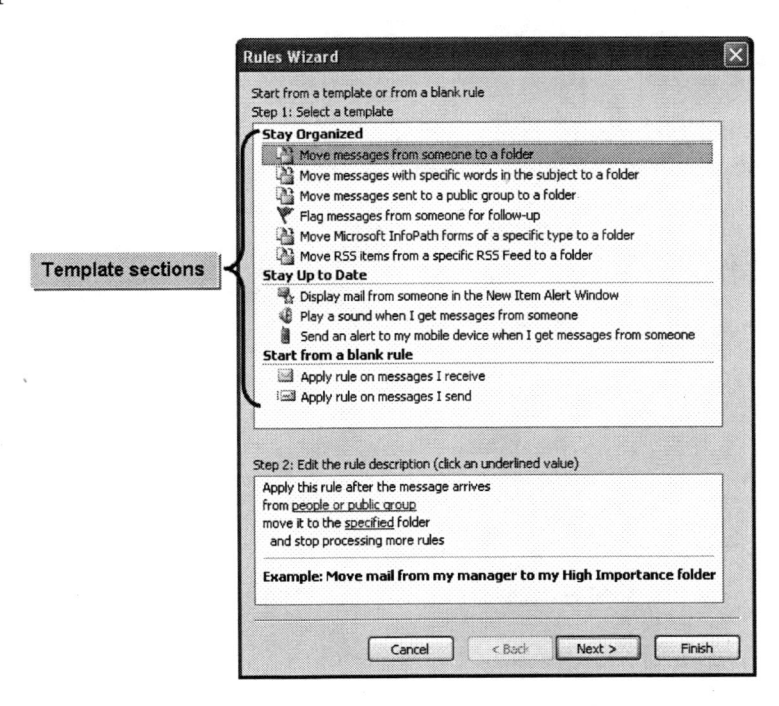

Figure 2-11: The predefined templates in the Rules Wizard.

Template Section	Description
Stay Organized	Contains rules that will help you file and follow up on messages.
Stay Up to Date	Contains rules that will notify you in some way when you receive a particular message.
Start from a blank rule	Allows you to create a new rule with custom criteria.

How to Organize Messages

Procedure Reference: Organize Messages Using Color

To organize messages using color:

1. Display the folder that contains messages you want to organize.
2. On the **View** tab, in the **Current View** group, click **View Settings**.
3. In the **Advanced View Settings** dialog box, click **Conditional Formatting**.
4. In the **Conditional Formatting** dialog box, click **Add** to add a new rule, and name it in the **Name** text box.
5. Click the **Font** option to open the **Font** dialog box.
6. From the **Color** drop-down list, select a color, make the other font changes as required, click **OK** to apply the changes, and close the **Font** dialog box.
7. In the **Conditional Formatting** dialog box, click **Condition** to set a condition for the messages.
8. In the **Filter** dialog box, select either **From** or **Sent To** and select the user name of the person whose messages you want displayed in color.
9. Click **OK** three times subsequently to close the dialog boxes.

> For more detailed formatting options, click **Automatic Formatting**.

Procedure Reference: Organize Messages Using Views

To organize messages using views:

1. Display the folder that contains messages you want to organize.
2. From the **View** tab, in the **Arrangement** group, choose a view.
3. The messages in the selected folder are displayed according to the view selected.

Procedure Reference: Remove Message Color

To remove message color:

1. Display the folder that contains messages you want to remove color from.
2. From the **View** tab, in the **Current View** group, click **View Settings**.
3. In the **Advanced View Settings** dialog box, click **Conditional Formatting**.

4. In the **Conditional Formatting** dialog box, select the rule that needs to be removed and click **Delete** to remove it.
5. Click **OK** to close **Conditional Formatting** dialog box.

Procedure Reference: Organize Messages Using the Rules Wizard

To organize messages using the Rules Wizard:
1. Display the folder that contains messages you want to organize.
2. On the **Home** tab, in the **Move** group, from the **Rules** drop-down list, choose **Manage Rules & Alerts.**
3. In the **Rules and Alerts** dialog box, click **New Rule** to display the **Rules Wizard.**
4. On the **Start from a template or from a blank rule** page, in the **Step 1: Select a template** list box, select an option, and then click **Next.**
5. On the **Which condition(s) do you want to check** page, in the **Step 1: Select condition(s)** list box, check the condition(s) you want to apply.
6. In the **Step 2: Edit the rule description (click an underlined value)** list box, click any underlined value, edit it, and then click **Next.**

> Most options that you select will have a value to edit. You can edit the values any time by clicking the underlined word in the **Rule Description** list box.

7. On the **What do you want to do with the message** page, in the **Step 1: Select action(s)** list box, check an option.
8. In the **Step 2: Edit the rule description (click an underlined value)** list box, edit any underlined values, and then click **Next.**
9. If necessary, on the **Are there any exceptions** page, in the **Step 1: Select exception(s) (If necessary)** list box, check an exception, and then click **Next.**
10. On the **Finish Rule Setup** page, in the **Step 1: Specify a name for this rule** text box, type a name for the rule.
11. If necessary, set up a rule option.
    - Check the **Run this rule now on messages already in** [Outlook folder] check box to apply the rule for the messages that were already in the specific Outlook folder.
    - If necessary, check the **Turn on this rule** check box to apply the rule to future email items.

> The **Turn On This Rule** check box is checked by default.

12. Click **Finish** to create the rule and close the **Rules Wizard.**
13. In the **Rule** list box, select the rule and click **OK** to apply the rule and close the **Rules And Alerts** dialog box.

Procedure Reference: Create a Rule to Delete All Email Messages from a Sender

To create a rule for deleting all email messages from a sender:
1. Display the Inbox folder.

2. Right-click the mail message from a user whose emails you want to delete and choose **Rules→ Create Rule.**
3. In the **Create Rule** dialog box, in the **When i get e-mail with all of the selected conditions** section, check the **From** [User name] check box.
4. In the **Do the following** section, check the **Move the item to folder** check box, and click **Select Folder** to display the **Rules and Alerts** dialog box.
5. Select the **Deleted Items** folder and click **OK** to close the **Rules and Alerts** dialog box.
6. Click **OK** to close the **Create Rule** dialog box.
7. In the **Success** warning box, check the **Run this rule now on messages already in the current folder** check box to apply the rule for the messages that were already in the current Outlook folder and click **OK** to apply the rule.

Procedure Reference: Create a Rule to Delete Email Messages

To create a rule to delete email messages:
1. Display the Inbox folder.
2. On the **Home** tab, in the **Move** group, click **Rules** and select **Manage Rules & Alerts** to display the **Rules and Alerts** dialog box.
3. In the **Rules and Alerts** dialog box, click **New rule** to display the Rules Wizard.
4. On the **Start from a template or from a blank rule** page, in the **Step 1: Select a template** list box, select an option, and then click **Next**.
5. On the **Which condition(s) do you want to check** page, in the **Step 1: Select condition(s)** list box, check the condition(s).

> The conditions include options to search for specific words in the subject or body, message header, recipient's address, sender's address, and more.

6. In the **Step 2: Edit the rule description (click an underlined value)** list box, click any underlined value, edit it, and then click **Next**.
7. On the **What do you want to do with the message** page, in the **Step 1: Select action(s)** list box, select **Delete it**, and then click **Next**.
8. If necessary, on the **Are there any exceptions** page, in the **Step 1: Select exception(s) (if necessary)** list box, check an exception, and then click **Next**.
9. On the **Finish rule setup** page, in the **Step 1: Specify a name for this rule** text box, type a name for the rule.
10. If necessary, set up a rule option.
11. Click **Finish** to create the rule and close the Rules Wizard.
12. In the **Rule** list box, select the rule and click **OK** to apply the rule and close the **Rules and Alerts** dialog box.

Procedure Reference: Create a Rule to Categorize Email Messages

To create a rule for categorizing email messages:
1. Display the Inbox folder.
2. Display the **Rules and Alerts** dialog box.
3. In the **Rules and Alerts** dialog box, click **New rule** to display the Rules Wizard.

4. On the **Start from a template or from a blank rule** page, in the **Step 1: Select a template** list box, select an option, and then click **Next**.
5. On the **Which condition(s) do you want to check** page, in the **Step 1: Select condition(s)** list box, check the condition(s).

> The conditions include options to search for specific words in the body, subject or body, message header, recipient's address, sender's address, and more.

6. In the **Step 2: Edit the rule description (click an underlined value)** list box, click any underlined value, edit it, and then click **Next**.
7. Assign a color category to the rule.
   a. On the **What Do You Want To Do With The Message** page, in the **Step 1: Select Action(s)** list box, check the **Assign it to the Category** check box.
   b. In the **Step 2: Edit the rule description (click an underlined value)** list box, click the **category** link.
   c. In the **Color categories** dialog box, click **New.**
   d. In the **Add New Category** dialog box, in the **Name** text box, type a color category name.
   e. From the **Color** drop-down list, select a color and click **OK.**
   f. In the **Color Categories** dialog box, click **OK.**
8. Click **Next.**
9. If necessary, on the **Are there any exceptions** page, in the **Step 1: Select exception(s) (if necessary)** list box, check an exception, and then click **Next.**
10. On the **Finish rule setup** page, in the **Step 1: Specify a name for this rule** text box, type a name for the rule.
11. If necessary, set up a rule option.
12. Click **Finish** to create the rule and close the Rules Wizard.
13. In the **Rule** list, select the rule and click **OK** to apply the rule and close the **Rules and Alerts** dialog box.

Procedure Reference: Create a Rule to Forward Email Messages

To create a rule for forwarding email messages:
1. Display the Inbox folder.
2. Display the **Rules and Alerts** dialog box.
3. In the **Rules and Alerts** dialog box, click **New rule** to display the Rules Wizard.
4. On the **Start from a template or from a blank rule** page, in the **Step 1: Select a template** list box, select the option that allows you to forward email messages, and then click **Next.**
5. On the **Which condition(s) do you want to check** page, in the **Step 1: Select condition(s)** list box, check the condition(s).

> The conditions include options to search for specific words in the subject or body, message header, recipient's address, sender's address, and more.

6. In the **Step 2: Edit the rule description (click an underlined value)** list box, click any underlined value, edit it, and then click **Next.**
7. On the **What do you want to do with the message** page, in the **Step 1: Select action(s)** list box, check the **Forward it to people or public group** check box.
8. In the **Step 2: Edit the rule description (Click An Underlined Value)** list box, click the **People or distribution** List link.
9. In the **Rule** Address dialog box, in the **To** field, add the user name to whom you want to forward the messages, and then click **OK.**
10. Click **Next.**
11. If necessary, on the **Are there any exceptions** page, in the **Step 1: Select exception(s) (if necessary)** list box, check an exception, and then click **Next.**
12. On the **Finish rule setup** page, in the **Step 1: Specify a name for this rule** text box, type a name for the rule.
13. If necessary, set up a rule option.
14. Click **Finish** to create the rule and close the Rules Wizard.
15. In the **Rule** list, select the rule and click **OK** to apply the rule and close the **Rules and Alerts** dialog box.

Procedure Reference: Delete a Rule

To delete a rule:
1. Display the **Rules and Alerts** dialog box.
2. In the **Rule (Applied In The Order Shown)** list box, select the rule you want to delete and click **Delete.**
3. In the **Microsoft Outlook** warning box, click **Yes** to delete the rule.
4. Click **OK** to close the **Rules and Alerts** dialog box.

Procedure Reference: Categorize Contact Information Using Color

To categorize contact information using color:
1. Display the Contacts folder that contains contacts you want to categorize.
2. Double-click a contact to display the Contact form.
3. On the **Contact Group** tab, in the **Tags** group, click **Categorize** and select **All Categories.**
4. In the **Color Categories** dialog box, click **New.**
5. In the **Add New Category** dialog box, in the **Name** text box, type a name for the new color category.
6. From the **Color** drop-down list, select a color and click **OK.**
7. In the **Color Categories** dialog box, click **OK** to assign a color category for the contact.
8. In the **Actions** group, click **Save & Close** to close the Contact form.

Procedure Reference: Categorize Appointments or Meetings Using Color

To categorize appointments or meetings using color:
1. Display the Calendar folder that contains appointments or meetings you want to categorize.
2. Double-click an appointment or meeting to display the Appointment or Meeting form.

3. On the **Appointment** or **Contact** tab, in the **Options** group, click **Categorize** and select **All Categories.**
4. In the **Color Categories** dialog box, click **New.**
5. In the **Add New Category** dialog box, in the **Name** text box, type a name for the new color category.
6. From the **Color** drop-down list, select a color and click **OK.**
7. In the **Color Categories** dialog box, click **OK** to assign a color category for the contact.
8. In the **Actions** group, click **Save & Close** to close the Contact form.

ACTIVITY 2-6
Organizing Messages Using Color and Views

Scenario:
You are working on an important sales opportunity and want to make sure that any email messages from a particular customer are addressed promptly. To help ensure that you do not overlook these messages, you decide to color-code messages in your Inbox so that any messages received from this customer will be displayed in red. To quickly review the email that you have sent, you also want to display the messages in your Inbox in the order they were received.

1. Color-code messages from a particular sender in red.

    a. Display the Inbox folder.

    b. On the **View** tab, in the **Current View** group, click **View Settings.**

    c. In the **Advanced View Settings: Compact** dialog box, click the **Conditional Formatting** option.

    d. In the **Conditional Formatting** dialog box, click **Add** to add a new rule, and in the **Name** text box, type *Red*

    e. Click the **Font** option to open the **Font** dialog box.

    f. From the **Color** drop-down list, select **Red** and click **OK** to apply the changes, and to close the **Font** dialog box.

    > In the **Font** dialog box, the other formatting changes may be made as desired.

    g. In the **Conditional Formatting** dialog box, select the **Condition** option.

    h. In the **Filter** dialog box, enter the name of your partner in the **From** text box.

    i. Click **OK** three times subsequently to close the dialog boxes.

j. Observe that the messages from your partner in the Inbox, are displayed in Red.

2. Display your Inbox messages in the order they were received.

   a. On the **View** tab, in the **Arrangement** group, click **To** to view the messages in the order that they were received.

   b. Observe the messages that were received from your partners are displayed in the **To** view in the order that they were received.

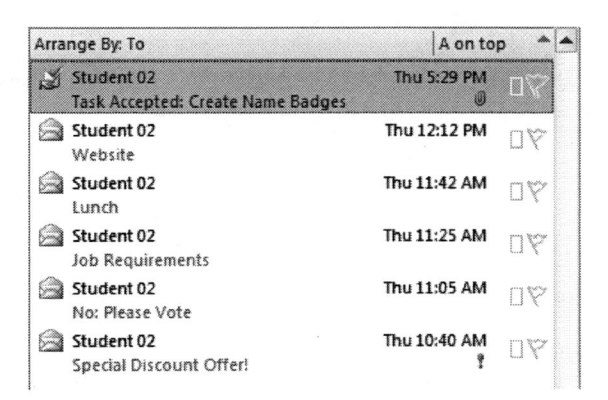

Arrange By: To	A on top
Student 02 — Task Accepted: Create Name Badges	Thu 5:29 PM
Student 02 — Website	Thu 12:12 PM
Student 02 — Lunch	Thu 11:42 AM
Student 02 — Job Requirements	Thu 11:25 AM
Student 02 — No: Please Vote	Thu 11:05 AM
Student 02 — Special Discount Offer!	Thu 10:40 AM

   c. On the Ribbon, click the **Home** tab.

Lesson 2: Organizing and Locating Messages   77

Microsoft® Office Outlook® 2010: Level 2

ACTIVITY 2-7
Organizing Messages Using the Rules Wizard

Setup:
The Inbox folder is displayed.

Scenario:
You are working on a project and you want the messages of a particular client to be stored in a new folder called Client X, so that it would be easier for future reference.

1. Remove the message coloring.

    a. On the **View** tab, in the **Current View** group, click **View Settings**.

    b. In the **Advanced View Settings: Compact** dialog box, click the **Conditional Formatting** button.

    c. In the **Conditional Formatting** dialog box, in the **Rules for this view** list, select **Red** and click **Delete**.

    d. Click **OK** twice.

2. Create a new folder called Client X as a subfolder within your Inbox folder.

    a. On the **Folder** tab, in the **New** group, click **New Folder**.

    b. In the **Create New Folder** dialog box, in the **Name** text box, type **Client X** and click **OK**.

    c. Observe that the **Client X** subfolder is displayed within your **Inbox**.

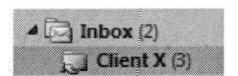

    ▲ 📥 Inbox (2)
    　　📁 Client X (3)

3. Use the Rules Wizard to create the rule.

    a. On the **Home** tab, in the **Move** group, from the **Rules** drop-down list, select **Manage Rules & Alerts**.

    b. In the **Rules and Alerts** dialog box, click **New Rule** to display the **Rules Wizard**.

78　Lesson 2: Organizing and Locating Messages

c. On the **Start from a template or from a blank rule** page, in the **Step 1: Select a template** list box, verify that the **Move messages from someone to a folder** option is selected, and click **Next**.

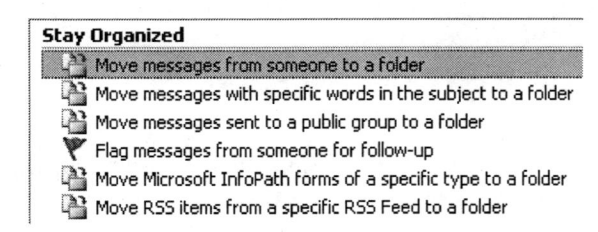

> **Stay Organized**
> Move messages from someone to a folder
> Move messages with specific words in the subject to a folder
> Move messages sent to a public group to a folder
> Flag messages from someone for follow-up
> Move Microsoft InfoPath forms of a specific type to a folder
> Move RSS items from a specific RSS Feed to a folder

d. On the **Which condition(s) do you want to check** page, in the **Step 2: Edit the rule description (click an underlined value)** list box, click the **people or public group** link.

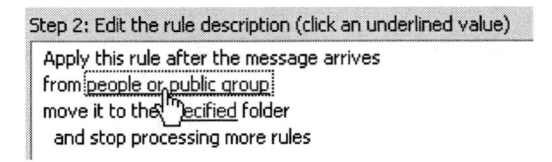

> Step 2: Edit the rule description (click an underlined value)
> Apply this rule after the message arrives
> from people or public group
> move it to the specified folder
> and stop processing more rules

e. In the **Rule Address** dialog box, in the list of addresses, select your partner and click **From**.

f. Click **OK** and then click **Next**.

g. On the **What do you want to do with the message** page, in the **Step 2: Edit the rule description (click an underlined value)** list box, click the **specified** link.

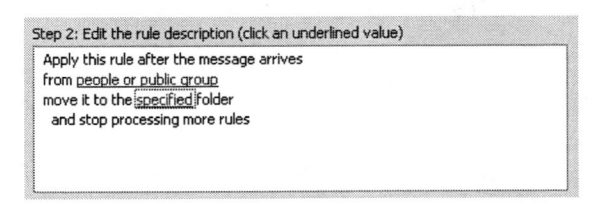

> Step 2: Edit the rule description (click an underlined value)
> Apply this rule after the message arrives
> from people or public group
> move it to the specified folder
> and stop processing more rules

h. In the **Rules and Alerts** dialog box, expand the **Inbox** folder and click **Client X**.

i. Click **OK** and then click **Next**.

j. On the **Are there any exceptions** page, click **Next** to bypass the Exceptions page.

k. On the **Finish rule setup** page, in the **Step 1: Specify a name for this rule** text box, replace the existing text with *My Rule*

l. In the **Step 2: Setup rule options** section, check the **Run this rule now on messages already in "Inbox"** check box and click **Finish**.

m. Click **OK** to apply the rule and close the **Rules And Alerts** dialog box.

n. In the Navigation pane, select the **Client X** folder.

o. Observe that the messages from your partner have been moved.

ACTIVITY 2-8
Creating a Rule to Categorize Email Messages

Scenario:
Working on an important business prospect, you want to automatically organize all the email messages that you received from one of your clients for easy identification and reference.

1. Add the client to the **From** text box of the **Rule Address** dialog box.

    a. On the **Home** tab, in the **Move** group, from the **Rules** drop-down list, select **Manage Rules & Alerts**.

    b. In the **Rules And Alerts** dialog box, **click New Rule** to display the **Rules Wizard**.

    c. On the **Start from a template or from a blank rule** page, in the **Step 1: Select a template** list box, in the **Start from a blank rule** section, select **Apply rule on messages I receive** and click **Next**.

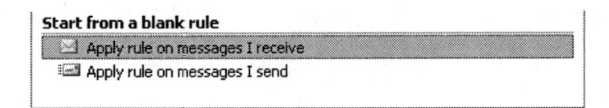

    d. On the **Which condition(s) do you want to check** page, in the **Step 1: Select condition(s)** list box, check the **from people or public group** check box.

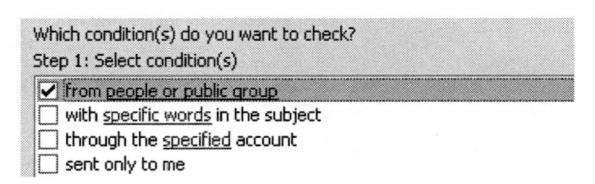

    e. In the **Step 2: Edit the rule description (click an underlined value)** list box, click the **people or public group** link.

    f. In the **Rule Address** dialog box, in the **From** text box, add your partner, click **OK** and then click **Next**.

2. Create a rule to organize email messages that are received from the client.

    a. On the **What do you want to do with the message** page, in the **Step 1: Select action(s)** list box, check the **assign it to the category category** check box.

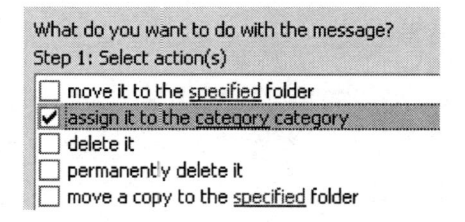

Lesson 2: Organizing and Locating Messages

b. In the **Step 2: Edit the rule description (click an underlined value)** list box, click the **category** link.

c. In the **Color Categories** dialog box, click **New.**

d. In the **Add New Category** dialog box, in the **Name** text box, type *Emails From Client* to assign a name for the new color category.

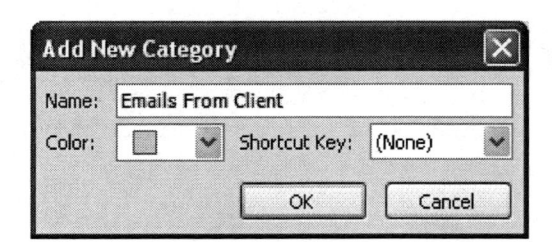

e. From the **Color** drop-down list, in the first row, select the desired color and click **OK**.

f. In the **Color Categories** dialog box, click **OK,** and then click **Next.**

g. On the **Are there any exceptions** page, click **Next** to bypass the Exceptions page.

h. On the **Finish Rule Setup** page, in the **Step 1: Specify a name for this rule** text box, replace the existing text with *My Email Rule*

i. In the **Step 2: Setup rule options** section, check the **Run this rule now on messages already in "Client X"** check box and click **Finish.**

j. Click **OK** to apply the rule and close the subsequent dialog box.

ACTIVITY 2-9
Creating a Rule to Forward Email Messages

Scenario:
As a project manager, you regularly interface with one of your external clients on project-related issues. You receive a lot of email from the client, and instead of manually forwarding these email messages to your team member, you decide to create a rule to take care of this task.

1. Add your instructor to the **From** text box.

   a. On the **Home** tab, in the **Move** group, from the **Rules** drop-down list, select **Manage Rules & Alerts.**

   b. In the **Rules and Alerts** dialog box, click **New Rule** to display the **Rules Wizard.**

   c. On the **Start from a template or from a blank rule** page, in the **Step 1: Select a template** list box, in the **Start from a blank rule** section, select **Apply rule on messages I receive** and click **Next.**

   d. On the **Which condition(s) do you want to check** page, in the **Step 1: Select condition(s)** list box, check the **from people or public group** check box.

   e. In the **Step 2: Edit the rule description (click an underlined value)** list box, click the **people or public group** link.

   f. In the **Rule address** dialog box, in the **From** text box, add your instructor **Student 00**, click **OK** and then click **Next.**

2. Create a rule to forward email messages.

   a. On the **What do you want to do with the message** page, from the **Step 1: Select action(s)** list box, check the **forward it to people or public group** check box.

   b. In the **Step 2: Edit the rule description (click an underlined value)** list box, click the **people or public group** link.

   c. In the **Rule Address** dialog box, in the **To** text box, add your partner to whom you want to forward the messages. Click **OK** and then click **Next.**

   d. On the **Are there any exceptions** page, click **Next** to bypass the Exceptions page.

   e. On the **Finish rule setup** page, in the **Step 1: Specify a name for this rule** text box, replace the existing text with *My Rule 2*

   f. In the **Step 2: Setup Rule Options** section, check the **Run this rule now on messages already in "Inbox"** check box.

   g. Click **Finish** and then click **OK** to apply the rule and close the **Rules and Alerts** dialog box.

TOPIC F
Manage Junk Email

You sorted your Inbox, set rules, and organized your messages in various ways. While organizing your messages, you might find some unwanted junk email messages in your Inbox. In this topic, you will review and set Outlook's junk email options.

With so much junk email flooding the Internet these days, it is inevitable that, at some point, you will receive some of them. Because it gives you frustration and a potential virus threat, Outlook provides some help by offering options that allow you to set a level of protection from junk email or add names to a trusted sender list.

Spam

Spam is unsolicited email advertising for a product that is sent to an individual, mailing list, or newsgroup. It usually comes from fake email addresses.

Junk E-Mail Filter

The *Junk E-Mail Filter* automatically filters every incoming message to determine if it is a suspicious or fraudulent email. Filtered junk messages are stored in the Junk E-Mail folder, so that they can be reviewed at any time to make sure that they are not legitimate messages that you do want to receive. This feature of filtering junk emails can be applied using the **Junk E-mail Options** dialog box. By default, the Junk E-mail Filter is turned on and the protection level set to Low.

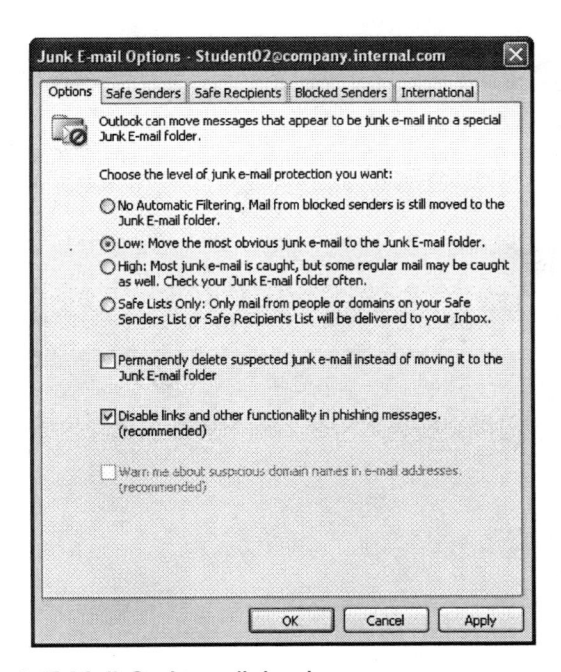

Figure 2-12: The Junk E-Mail Options dialog box.

Blocked Senders List

The **Blocked Senders** list consists of email addresses or domain names of contacts whose messages you want to block. You can block email messages from certain senders by adding their email addresses or domain names to the **Blocked Senders** list. When you receive messages from blocked senders, they are treated as junk and moved to the Junk E-Mail folder.

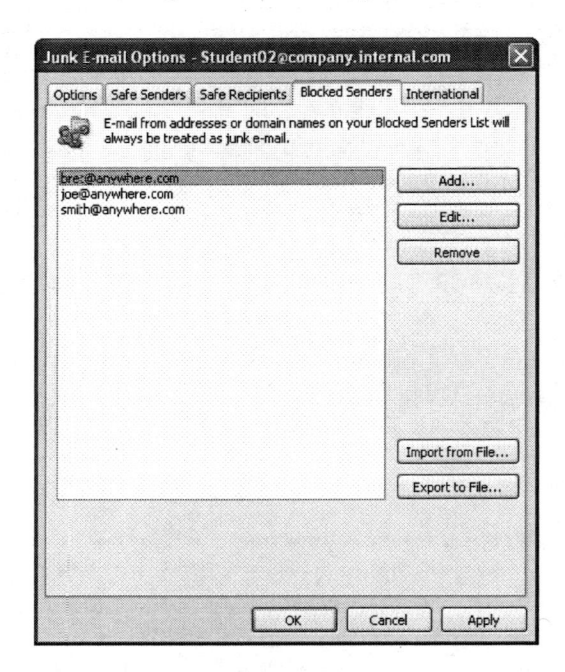

Figure 2-13: Email addresses of blocked contacts in the Blocked Senders list.

> You can export the email addresses of users if you want to print copies of the **Blocked Senders** list.

Safe Senders List

The **Safe Senders** list consists of email addresses or domain names of contacts whose messages you want delivered to your Inbox. Certain messages may be mistakenly marked junk by the Junk E-mail Filter. By adding the email addresses or domain names of senders to the **Safe Senders** list, messages received from those senders are listed in the Inbox and not in the Junk E-Mail folder.

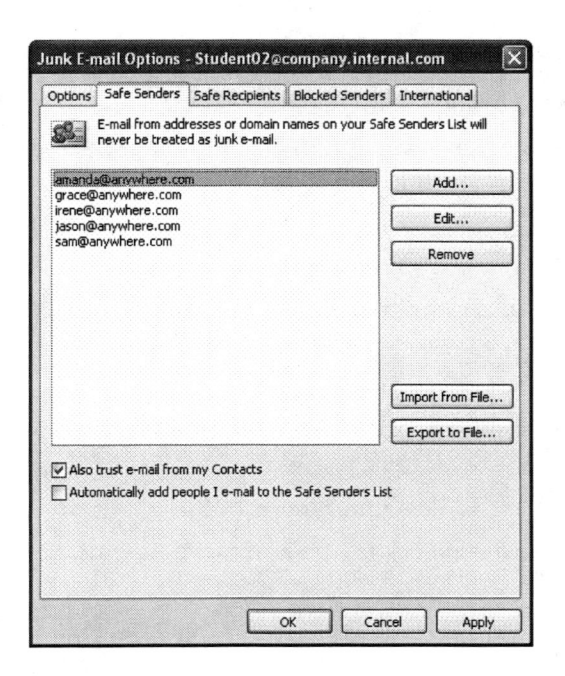

Figure 2-14: Email addresses of safe contacts in the Safe Senders list.

> The email addresses in your **Contacts** list are considered safe by the Junk E-Mail filter if the **Also Trust e-mail From my Contacts** option is selected. You may send email to people who are not listed in your **Contacts** folder. If you consider these addresses to be safe, select **Automatically add people I e-mail to the Safe Senders List**

How to Manage Junk Email

Procedure Reference: Manage the Safe Senders List

To manage the Safe Senders list:

1. Display the **Junk E-mail Options** dialog box.
   - On the Ribbon, on the **Home** tab, in the **Delete** group, from the **Junk** drop-down list, select **Junk E-mail Options** or;
   - Right-click an email message, and from the displayed menu, choose **Junk→Junk E-mail Options.**
2. In the **Junk E-mail Options** dialog box, on the **Options** tab, select the level of junk email protection that you need and set other options relating to junk email messages.
3. On the **Safe Senders** tab, click **Add.**
4. In the **Add address or domain** text box, enter an email address or domain name that needs to be added to the list.
5. Click **OK** to add the address or domain to the list.
6. If necessary, on the **Safe Senders** tab, edit, remove, import, or export email addresses or domain names.
7. Similarly, on the Safe Recipients tab, specify the options.
8. Close the **Junk E-mail Options** dialog box.

Procedure Reference: Manage the Block Senders List

To manage the Block Senders list:

1. Display the **Junk E-mail Options** dialog box.
   - On the Ribbon, on the **Home** tab, in the **Delete** group, from the **Junk** drop-down list, select **Junk E-mail Options** or;
   - Right-click an email message, and from the displayed menu, choose **Junk→Junk E-mail Options.**
2. In the **Junk E-mail Options** dialog box, on the **Options** tab, select the level of junk email protection that you need and set other options relating to junk email messages.
3. On the **Blocked Senders** tab, click **Add.**
4. In the **Add address or domain** text box, enter the email address or domain name to be added to the list.
5. Click **OK** to add the address or domain to the list.
6. If necessary, on the **Blocked Senders** tab, edit, remove, import, or export email addresses or domain names.
7. On the **International** tab, set the options to block countries, regions, and specific encoding formats to ensure that these email messages will always be treated as junk.
   1. Block all messages sent from an email address ending with a specific top-level domain.
      a. Click **Blocked Top-Level Domain List.**
      b. In the **Blocked Top-Level Domain List** dialog box, check the desired check boxes to add the countries or regions to the domain list.
      c. Click **OK** to add the address or domain to the list.
   2. Block all email messages in specific encoding formats.
      a. Click **Blocked Encodings List.**
      b. In the **Blocked Encodings List** dialog box, check one or more encoding formats to be added to the list.
      c. Click **OK** to add the address or domain to the list.
8. Close the **Junk E-mail Options** dialog box.

Procedure Reference: Mark a Message as Not Junk

To mark a message as not junk:

1. Display the Junk E-Mail folder.
2. Display the **Mark As Not Junk** dialog box.
   - Right-click a message, and from the displayed menu, choose **Junk E-mail→Mark As Not Junk** or;
   - Select a message, and on the **Home** tab, in the **Delete** group, from the **Junk** drop-down list, select **Not Junk.**
3. Click **OK** to restore the message to its original folder.

Procedure Reference: Empty the Junk E-Mail Folder

To empty the Junk E-Mail folder:

1. Right-click the Junk E-Mail folder and choose **Empty Folder.**

2. In the **Microsoft Outlook** message box, click **Yes** to permanently delete all messages and folders in the Junk E-Mail folder.

ACTIVITY 2-10
Managing Junk Email Messages

Scenario:
You have been receiving a lot of junk email messages from the website **www.citizensinfo.org**. Because Outlook has a junk email filter, you want to filter any email message from this website, and automatically move it to the Junk E-Mail folder. You also notice that the email messages that you receive from a friend are being moved to the Junk E-Mail folder. Therefore, you want to add his email address to the list of trusted email addresses so that they are delivered to the Inbox, and not to the Junk E-Mail folder. Also, sometimes email messages from people you regularly correspond with get moved to the Junk E-Mail folder, and you want these email messages to be delivered to the Inbox.

1. Add www.citizensinfo.org to the Blocked Senders list.

   a. On the **Home** tab, in the **Delete** group, from the **Junk** drop-down list, select **Junk E-mail Options** to display the **Junk E-mail Options** dialog box.

   b. In the **Junk E-mail Options** dialog box, select the **Blocked Senders** tab and click **Add**.

   c. In the **Add address or domain** dialog box, in the text box, type *citizensinfo.org* and click **OK**.

   d. Observe that the citizensinfo.org domain is added to the Blocked Senders list.

2. Add the email address justin@ogc.example to the Safe Senders list.

   a. In the **Junk E-mail Options** dialog box, select the **Safe Senders** tab and click **Add**.

   b. In the **Add address or domain** dialog box, in the text box, type *justin@ogc.example* and click **OK**.

   c. Observe that the **justin@ogc.example** email address is added to the Safe Senders list.

d. Below the Safe Senders list box, check the **Automatically add people I e-mail to the Safe Senders List** check box to ensure that the email messages from the people you correspond with are delivered to the Inbox.

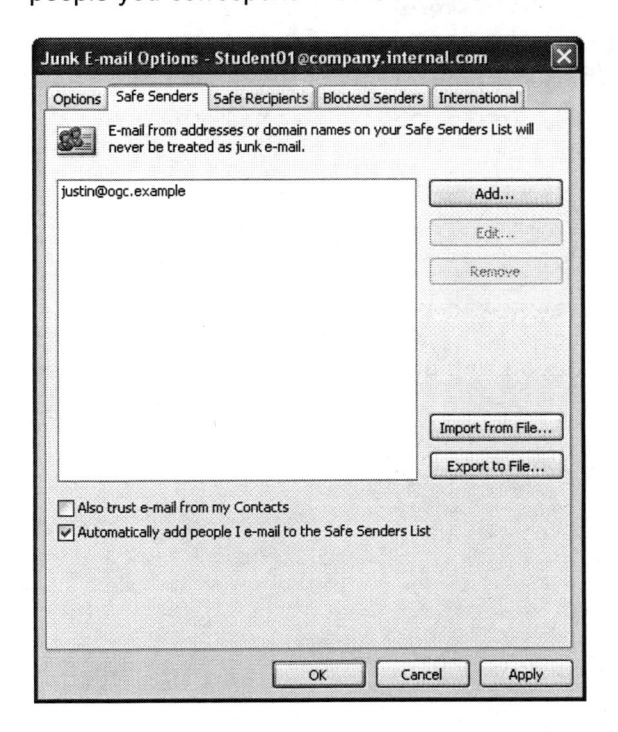

e. In the **Junk E-mail Options** dialog box, click **Apply,** and then click **OK.**

Lesson 2 Follow-up

In this lesson, you organized and located Outlook messages using the advanced features of Outlook. Now you can organize, sort, find, and filter Outlook items to quickly locate and display messages, and you can color-code messages to categorize and highlight them.

1. **Given the various ways to locate Outlook items, which ones are you most likely to use?**

2. **What are the reasons that compel you to manage your junk-email messages?**

3 | Setting Calendar Options

Lesson Time: 30 minutes

Lesson Objectives:

In this lesson, you will set calendar options.

You will:

- Set workdays and time in the calendar.
- Display an additional time zone on your calendar.
- Set availability options.
- Create a Calendar group.
- Manage automatic meeting responses.

Introduction

You used advanced search options to efficiently locate Outlook items. You also know that an electronic calendar can help you keep your work schedule up-to-date by displaying workdays and time, appointments, meetings, and events. While Outlook provides a default calendar, it may not reflect all of your company's requirements. In this lesson, you will set various calendar options.

You may plan your workdays and time using the Outlook Calendar defaults. But what if your company's work hours differ from the default, or you correspond with international clients and need to be aware of the time differences? By setting the appropriate calendar options, you can accommodate these and other needs.

TOPIC A
Set Workdays and Time

You are familiar with setting and customizing message options in Outlook. You may also want to customize some of Outlook's default calendar settings. In this topic, you will modify workdays and time, and include company holidays in the calendar.

Assume that you are the human resources manager of a company. You may have to schedule meeting days and time, or attend meetings with different companies. Setting the calendar workdays and time to reflect your company's needs is an important step in ensuring accurate scheduling.

Calendar Options

Outlook provides various options for customizing calendar settings, such as workhours and time zones. You can access these options from various sections of the **Calendar** tab, in the **Outlook Options** dialog box.

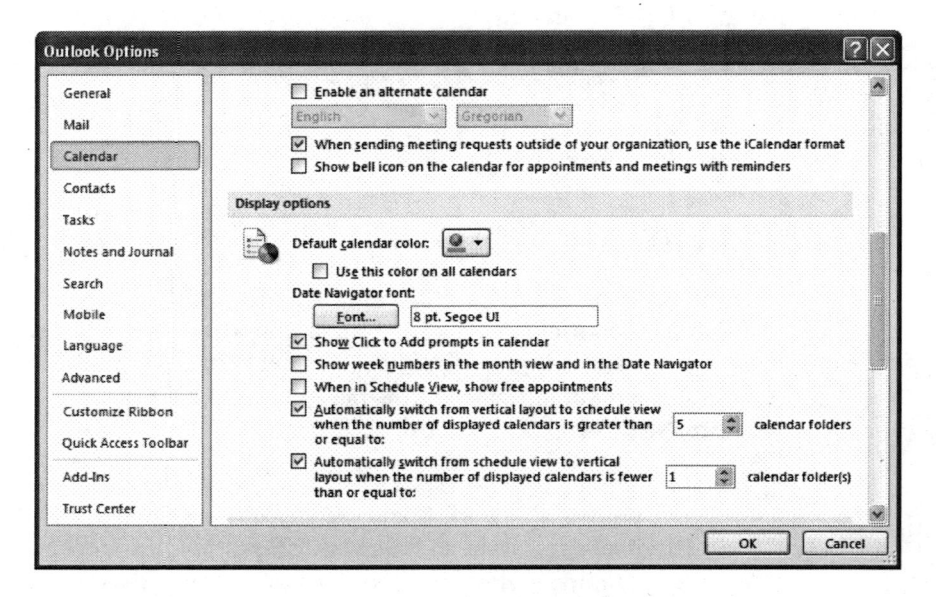

Figure 3-1: The Calendar Tab in the Outlook Options dialog box.

Section	Used for
Work time	Specifying **Work hours** and **Work week**, the **First day of week** and the **First week of year**, as well as **Start time** and **End time**.
Calendar options	Setting reminders, allowing meeting attendees to propose new time for meetings, setting **Free/Busy Options** and adding holidays.
Display options	Changing the way the calendar is displayed.
Time zones	Adding time zone information.

Section	Used for
Scheduling assistant	Displaying calendar details in the ScreenTip or in the scheduling grid.
Resource scheduling	Managing resources such as conference rooms, and accepting or declining meeting requests.

Internet Calendar Subscriptions

You can subscribe to and download a calendar from a calendar publishing service or a website, and view it in Outlook. Using these calendars, you can exchange calendar information between Outlook users regardless of the application being used to create or view the information. All Internet calendars use the iCalendar format with the .ICS file name extension. Once the calendar is downloaded and executed, it gets added to the Navigation pane in Calendar view under **Other Calendars** and opens side-by-side along with the default Outlook Calendar. The downloaded calendar checks for periodic updates made by the calendar publisher and automatically updates when it queries the server for updates. The websites that allow you to download calendars begin with the protocol *webcal://*.

How to Set Workdays and Time

Procedure Reference: Set Calendar Workdays and Time

To set calendar workdays and time:

1. On the Quick Launch bar, display the Calendar by clicking **Calendar.**
2. Select the **File** tab and click **Options** to display the **Outlook Options** dialog box.
3. In the **Outlook Options** dialog box, **Calendar** tab.
4. In the **Work time** section, set your calendar workweek options.
   - Set the workweek days by checking the appropriate check boxes.
   - Set the first day of your workweek by selecting the appropriate day from the **First day of week** drop-down list.
   - Set the first week of your work year by selecting the appropriate option from the **First week of year** drop-down list.
   - Set the start and end time for your workday by selecting the appropriate time from the **Start time** and **End time** drop-down lists.
5. Click **OK** to close the **Outlook Options** dialog box.

Procedure Reference: Add Holidays to the Calendar

To add holidays to the calendar:

1. Display the **Outlook Options** dialog box.
2. In the **Outlook Options** dialog box, select the **Calendar** tab, and in the **Calendar options** section, click **Add Holidays.**
3. In the **Add Holidays to Calendar** dialog box, check the check box next to the desired country to add the holidays of that country to the calendar.
4. Click **OK** to import the holidays into the calendar.
5. In the **Outlook Options** dialog box, click **OK** to close the dialog box.

Procedure Reference: Remove Holidays from Your Calendar

To remove holidays from your calendar:

1. With the Calendar displayed, on the **View** tab, in the **Current View** group, click **Change View** and select **List.**
2. Select the holidays that you want to remove, and press the delete key.
3. On the **View** tab, in the **Current View** group, click **Change View** and select **Calendar** to go back to the Calendar.

Microsoft® Office Outlook® 2010: Level 2

ACTIVITY 3-1
Setting Calendar Workdays, Time, and Holidays

Scenario:
Your Outlook calendar settings do not reflect the actual workdays—Monday through Saturday—and your work time, 8:30 AM to 5:30 PM. You also want the holiday details to be displayed in the calendar.

1. Display the Calendar.

    a. On the Quick Launch bar, click **Calendar** to switch to Calendar view.

    b. Observe that the starting time slot for working hours is 8:00 AM.

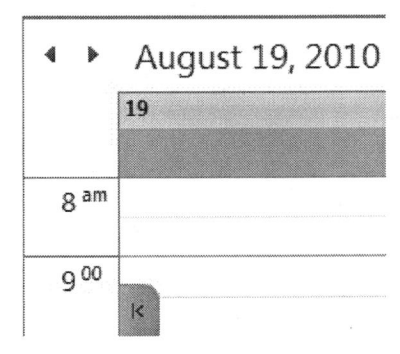

    c. On the **File** tab, choose **Options** to display the **Outlook Options** dialog box.

    d. In the **Outlook Options** dialog box, select the **Calendar** option.

2. Set Calendar options to reflect the company's workdays and hours.

    a. In the **Work time** section, from the **Start time** drop-down list, select **8:30 AM**.

    b. In the **End time** drop-down list, scroll down and select **5:30 PM**.

    c. In the **Work week** section, check the **Sat** check box.

    d. From the **First day of week** drop-down list, select **Monday** to set it as the first day of the work week.

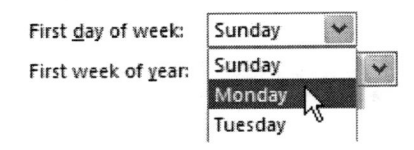

    e. Click **OK** to close the **Outlook Options** dialog box.

Lesson 3: Setting Calendar Options   95

f. Observe that the work time as well as the work week changes have been made in the calendar.

3. Verify that US holidays are displayed in the Calendar and save the settings.

   a. On the **File** tab, click **Options** to open the **Outlook Options** dialog box.

   b. Select the **Calendar** tab, and in the **Calendar options** section, click **Add Holidays**.

   c. In the **Add Holidays to Calendar** dialog box, verify that the **United States** check box is checked, and then click **OK** to return to the **Outlook Options** dialog box.

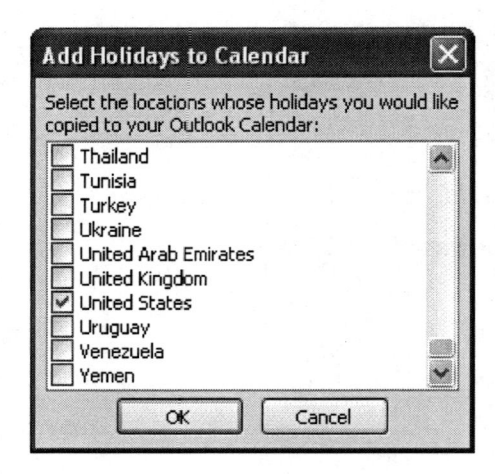

   d. In the Message box that appears, click **OK**.

   e. Click **OK** to save the new settings for the calendar and to close the **Outlook Options** dialog box.

   f. On the **View** tab, in the **Current View** group, click **Change View** and select **List** to view the added holidays.

   g. Observe that the holidays are added to the calendar.

TOPIC B
Display an Additional Time Zone

You have set workdays and time in your calendar. By default, the appointment section of your calendar displays your appointments in your correct time zone. But these days your clients are as likely to be across a continent as across a town, and noon on your schedule may be midnight for someone else. In this topic, you will display an additional time zone in your calendar.

Perhaps one of your biggest clients lives in a different time zone and you have to set up frequent and regular telephone conferences with him. To avoid scheduling a conference in the middle of the night for your client, you can display your client's time zone in your calendar.

The Additional Time Zone

In Outlook, the **Time zones** section is used to display the current time, day, and location. However, you can add and display a second time zone for use when you schedule meetings, appointments, and conference calls with associates located in differing time zones. When an additional time zone is added, the current time in the existing time zone is highlighted with a color gradient, which helps to differentiate the additional time zone from the current one. Having multiple time zones does not affect the way in which the calendar items are stored and displayed.

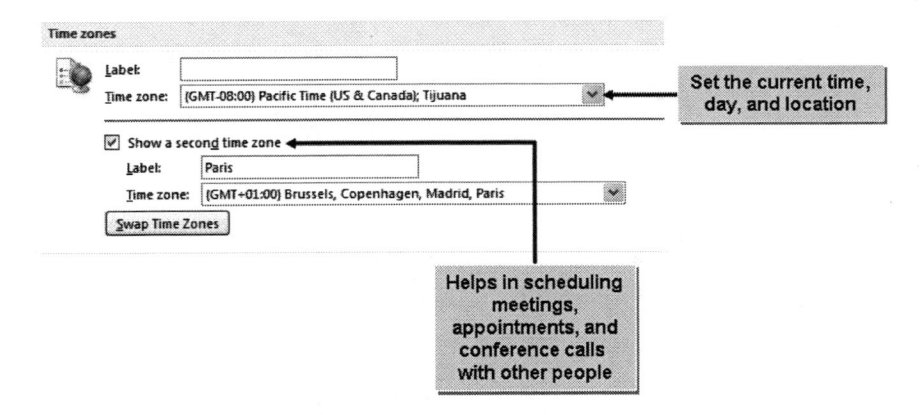

Figure 3-2: The Time zones section showing the second time zone.

How to Display an Additional Time Zone

Procedure Reference: Display an Additional Time Zone on your Calendar

To display an additional time zone on your calendar:

1. On the Quick Launch bar, click **Calendar** to display the Calendar.
2. Select the **File** tab and **Options** to display the **Outlook Options** dialog box.
3. In the **Outlook Options** dialog box, click **Calendar.**
4. In the **Time zones** section, check the **Show a second time zone** check box.
5. In the **Label** text box, enter a name for the new time zone.
6. From the **Time zone** drop-down list, select the desired time zone.
7. Click **OK** to close the **Outlook Options** dialog box.

ACTIVITY 3-2
Setting an Additional Time Zone

Scenario:
Your company is located in New York city but does a lot of business with clients in Paris. You want to avoid having to stop and calculate the time difference each time you place a call or schedule a conference call with these overseas clients.

1. Add a time zone for Paris.

    a. On the **File** tab, click **Options** to display the **Outlook Options** dialog box.

    b. In the **Outlook Options** dialog box, click **Calendar.**

    c. Scroll down and in the **Time zones** section, check the **Show a second time zone** check box.

    d. In the **Label** text box, type *Paris*

    e. From the **Time zone** drop-down list, select **(GMT+01:00) Brussels, Copenhagen, Madrid, Paris.**

    f. Click **OK** to close the **Outlook Options** dialog box.

    g. On the **View** tab, in the **Current View** group, click **Change View** and select **Calendar.**

h. Observe that an additional time zone is added and named **Paris**.

Paris	
6 pm	9 am
7 00	10 00
8 00	11 00
9 00	12 pm

2. **True or False? You can edit the Time zone option in Outlook to view a different time zone instead of the current one.**

   ___ True

   ___ False

TOPIC C
Set Availability Options

You are now familiar with setting an additional time zone in your calendar. Another calendar option that you may want to change is how much of your calendar information other users can see to check for your availability. In this topic, you will modify your calendar free and busy information.

Assume that you are working as a general manager in a company. Because coworkers would check your free and busy time when scheduling meetings, you may want to control how much of your calendar information is visible to them.

The Free/Busy Options Dialog Box

The **Free/Busy Options** dialog box allows you to modify the free and busy information in your calendar. To specify how many months of free and busy information is available on the server, you can enter the number of months in the **Publish** text box. You can also enter the time interval to specify how often the free and busy information on the server is updated.

In the **Internet Free/Busy** section, you can check the **Publish at my location** check box and specify the path of the server on which you will publish your free and busy data. The **Search location** option allows you to view the free or busy information for others, which can help you efficiently schedule meetings.

> Publishing the information on a server allows others to view your information.

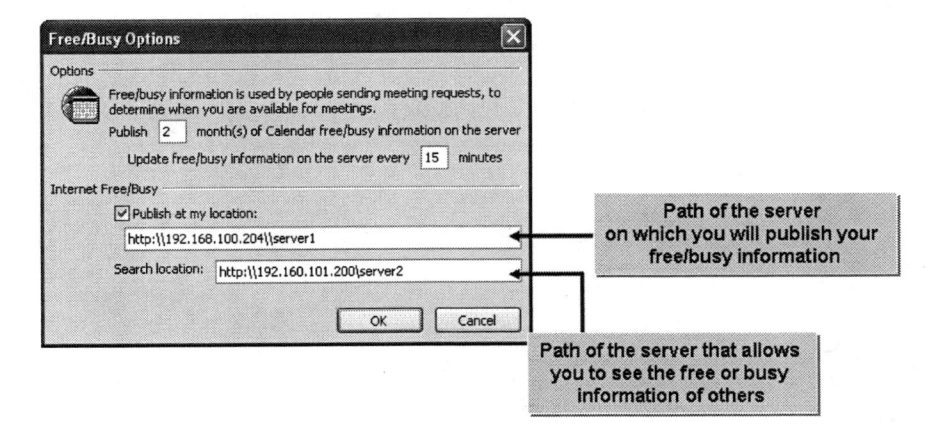

Figure 3-3: The Free/Busy dialog box that allows you to specify the information to be published on the server.

How to Set Availability Options

Procedure Reference: Modify Free/Busy Options

To modify calendar free/busy options:

1. On the Quick Launch bar, display the Calendar by clicking **Calendar.**
2. Select the **File** tab and click **Options** to display the **Outlook Options** dialog box.
3. In the **Outlook Options** dialog box, click **Calendar.**
4. In the **Calendar options** section, select the **Free/Busy Options** option.
5. On the **Permissions** tab, in the **Read** section of the **Permissions** section, click **Other Free/Busy.**
6. In the **Free/Busy Options** dialog box, type a number in the **Publish** text box to modify how many months of free/busy data is available on the server.

> While two months of calendar free/busy data is shown by default, users can publish a total of 36 months.

7. Type a number in the **Update free/busy information on the server every** text box to modify how often Outlook automatically updates your free/busy information on a server.
8. Click **OK** as necessary, to modify free/busy options and to close any open dialog boxes.

ACTIVITY 3-3
Modifying Free/Busy Information

Scenario:
As division manager, you have a series of upcoming one-on-one meetings that need to be scheduled over the next three months. You have asked each individual who needs to meet with you to schedule their own meeting. Therefore, you not only want three months of your calendar information posted to the server but also want the server to update the information every five minutes so that the most up-to-date information is posted frequently.

1. Set calendar free/busy options.

    a. Open the **Outlook Options** dialog box.

    b. In the **Outlook Options** dialog box, click **Calendar.**

    c. In the **Calendar options** section, select the **Free/Busy Options** option.

    d. On the **Permissions** tab, in the **Read** section of the **Permissions** section, click **Other Free/Busy.**

    e. In the **Free/Busy Options** dialog box, in the **Publish** text box, type *3*

    f. In the **Update free/busy information on the server every** text box, type *5*

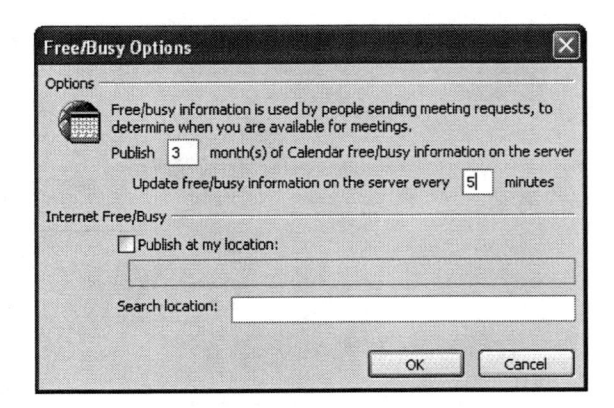

    g. Click **OK,** as necessary, to modify the settings and to close any open dialog boxes.

Lesson 3: Setting Calendar Options   103

2. **True or False? You can update the free/busy information on the server in Outlook.**
   ___ True
   ___ False

TOPIC D
Create Calendar Groups

You set your availability option by modifying your free or busy information. However, sometimes you may want to view and compare the combined schedule of individuals and arrange meetings with the entire group. In this topic, you will create Calendar groups.

Meetings are an inevitable part of professional interactions whether they occur face-to-face or virtually. You may have to schedule meetings, determine who will be attending them, and notify all invitees. By grouping the calendars of many individuals, you will be able to view and compare the combined availability of individuals and schedule meetings.

Calendar Groups

A *calendar group* is a collection of user calendars that allows participants to view and compare their schedules before scheduling a meeting. The **Calendar Groups** command can be accessed from the **Manage Calendars** group of the **Home** tab. You can create a calendar group of the currently displayed calendars using the **Save as New Calendar Group** command, or create a new calendar group using the **Create New Calendar Group** command.

Figure 3-4: The Calendar Groups button on the Calendar Home tab.

How to Create Calendar Groups
Procedure Reference: Create a Calendar Group

To create a Calendar group:

1. On the Quick Launch bar, display the Calendar by clicking **Calendar.**
2. On the **Home** tab, in the **Manage calendars** group, click **Calendar Groups** and select **Create New Calendar Group.**
3. In the **Create New Calendar Group** dialog box, enter a name for the Calendar group.
4. In the **Select Name: Global Address List** dialog box, in the **Name** list, select the names of contacts whose calendars you want to add to the calendar group.
5. Click **Group Members** and then click **OK** to apply the changes, and close the **Select Name: Global Address List** dialog box.

ACTIVITY 3-4
Creating a Calendar Group

Scenario:
You need to schedule a meeting with two of your project leads. Although you have their individual calendars, your job might become much easier if you create a calendar group to view their calendars, and compare their schedules. So you decide to create a calendar group.

1. Create a Calendar group.

    a. On the **Home** tab, in the **Manage Calendars** groups, click **Calendar Groups→Create New Calendar Group.**

    b. In the **Create New Calendar Group** dialog box, in the **Type a name for the new calendar group** text box, type *Project Leads* and click **OK.**

    c. In the **Select Name: Global Address List** dialog box, in the **Name** list, select the names of both your partners and click **OK.**

    d. Click **Group Members** and then click **OK** to apply the changes.

2. Which function can be performed by a Calendar group?

    a) Export a Calendar
    b) View Calendar holidays
    c) Set availability options
    d) View Calendars side by side

TOPIC E
Manage Automatic Meeting Responses

You created calendar groups to view and compare the calendars of a group of users. After sending the meeting request, it may be difficult for you to check whether users have accepted or declined your request. In this topic, you will manage automatic meeting responses.

Assume that in a typical week you schedule approximately 15 new meetings with different people. Your Inbox would be flooded with meeting responses from the people to whom you sent a meeting request. Outlook provides you with more convenient options to manage the meeting responses displayed in your Inbox.

How to Manage Automatic Meeting Responses
Procedure Reference: Generate Automatic Meeting Responses

To generate automatic meeting responses:

1. On the **Home** tab, in the **Move** group, from the **Rules** drop-down list, choose **Manage Rules & Alerts.**
2. In the **Rules and Alerts** dialog box, click **New Rule** to display the **Rules Wizard.**
3. On the **Start from a template or from a blank rule** page, in the **Step 1: Select a template** list box, select the **Apply rule on messages I receive** option, and click **Next.**
4. On the **Which condition(s) do you want to check** page, in the **Step 1: Select condition(s)** list box, check the **uses the form name form** check box.
5. In the **Step 2: Edit the rule description (click an underlined value)** list box, click **form name.**
6. From the drop-down at the top of the dialog box, select **Application Forms.**
7. In the list box, select **Accept Meeting Response** and click **Add** to add the form to the **Selected Forms** list.
8. In the list box, select **Tentative Meeting Response** and click **Add** to add the form to the **Selected Forms** list.
9. Click **Close** to close the **Choose Forms** dialog box, and in the **Rules Wizard,** click **Next.**
10. On the **What do you want to do with the message** page, from the **Step 1: Select action(s)** list box, check the **move it to the specified folder** option.
11. In the **Step 2: Edit the rule description (click an underlined value)** list box, click **specified,** specify a folder to which you want to move the responses and click **OK.**
12. Click **Finish** to create the rule and close the Rules Wizard.
13. In the **Rule** list, select the rule and click **OK** to apply the rule and close the **Rules And Alerts** dialog box.

Microsoft® Office Outlook® 2010: Level 2

ACTIVITY 3-5
Setting an Automatic Meeting Response

Scenario:
You need to schedule a meeting and send it to a large number of attendees. Since you are assuming that only a limited number of people are going to attend, you need the responses of those people who are either going to accept or tentatively accept the meeting request. So, you create a rule to refine your incoming requests based on those guidelines.

1. Set an Automatic Meeting response.

    a. Display the **Inbox** folder.

    b. On the **Home** tab, in the **Move** group, from the **Rules** drop-down list, choose **Manage Rules & Alerts**.

    c. In the **Rules and Alerts** dialog box, click **New Rule** to display the **Rules Wizard**.

    d. On the **Start from a template or from a blank rule** page, in the **Step 1: Select a template** list box, in the **Start from a blank rule** section, select **Apply rule on messages I receive**, and then click **Next**.

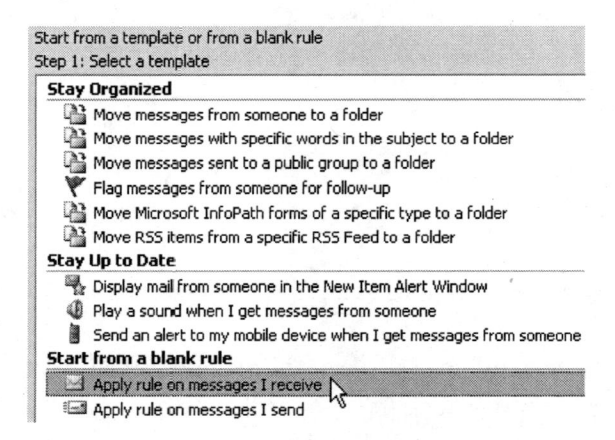

e. On the **Which condition(s) do you want to check** page, in the **Step 1: Select condition(s)** list box, scroll down and check the **uses the form name form** check box.

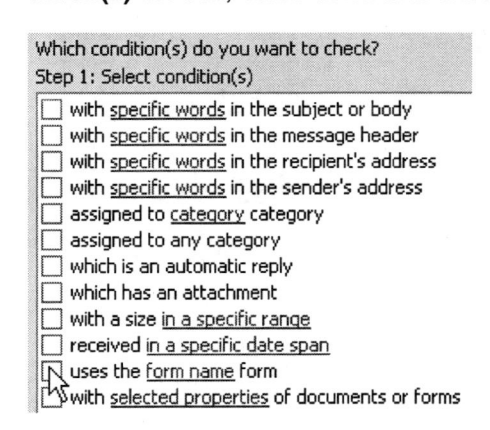

f. In the **Step 2: Edit the rule description (click an underlined value)** list box, click **form name.**

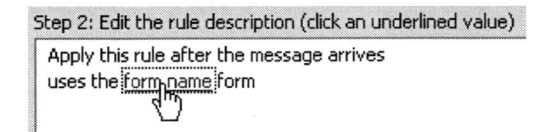

g. In the **Choose Forms** dialog box, from the drop-down list at the top of the dialog box, select **Application Forms.**

h. In the list box, select **Accept Meeting Response** and click **Add** to add the form to the **Selected Forms** list.

i. In the list box, scroll down select **Tentative Meeting Response** and click **Add** to add the form to the **Selected Forms** list.

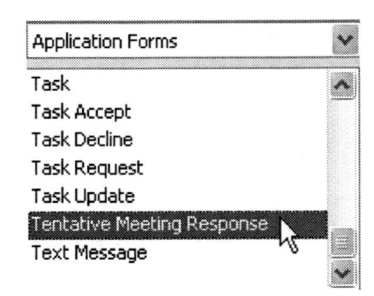

j. Click **Close** to close the **Choose Forms** dialog box.

k. In the **Rules Wizard,** click **Next.**

l. On the **What do you want to do with the message** page, in the **Step 1: Select action(s)** list box, check the **move it to the specified folder** check box.

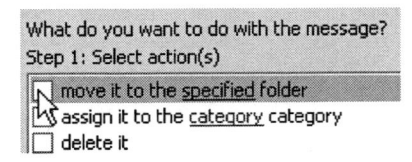

Lesson 3: Setting Calendar Options   109

m. In the **Step 2: Edit the rule description (click an underlined value)** list box, click the **specified** link to open the **Rules and Alerts** dialog box.

n. Verify that **Inbox** is selected and click **OK**.

o. Click **Finish** to create the rule and close the **Rules Wizard**.

p. In the **Rule** list, verify that the rule is selected, and click **OK** to apply the rule and close the **Rules And Alerts** dialog box.

2. **True or False? You can move the responses only to your Inbox.**

___ True

___ False

Lesson 3 Follow-up

In this lesson, you customized the calendar by setting various calendar options. By setting the appropriate calendar options, you can accommodate differences that may exist between the default calendar provided by Outlook and your specific needs.

1. **Which calendar options are you most likely to alter?**

2. **What business or personal reasons do you have for setting up multiple time zones in your calendar?**

4 Tracking Activities Using the Journal

Lesson Time: 30 minutes

Lesson Objectives:

In this lesson, you will track activities using the Journal.

You will:

- Automatically record a Journal entry.
- Manually record a Journal entry.
- Modify a Journal entry.

Introduction

You have set up calendar and message options. Although you may send email messages, make phone calls, schedule and attend appointments and meetings, and write numerous reports on a daily basis, at the end of a busy week, you may ask yourself, "What did I accomplish this week?" In this lesson, you will track activities with the Journal tool.

Accounting for one's time continues to be an important aspect in the workplace. While reviewing your calendar for the past week can help you determine how your time was spent, Outlook offers another tool, called the Journal, that automatically tracks and displays work activities in a timeline format.

Microsoft® Office Outlook® 2010: Level 2

TOPIC A
Record a Journal Entry Automatically

You set calendar options and corresponded with clients in different time zones. You may want to automatically record your work activities. Outlook offers a unique tool with which you can track items for certain contacts and Office application files. In this topic, you will use Outlook's Journal folder to automatically track your activities.

Although you can keep track of your work activities on paper or in your Outlook calendar, you can also take advantage of the Outlook Journal. Using the Journal, you can automatically record many of the interactions you perform, such as email messages that you send and receive, or work that you do on an Excel spreadsheet, or other Office applications.

The Journal

Definition:

The *Journal* is an Outlook tool that automatically records completed actions and displays them in a variety of timeline views. You can use the Journal to create journal entries that track email messages, meeting information, task requests, items for a specific contact, or a phone conversation. You can manually create journal entries that cannot be automatically recorded.

> You can also record files from other Microsoft Office applications such as Access, Excel, PowerPoint, and Word.

Example:

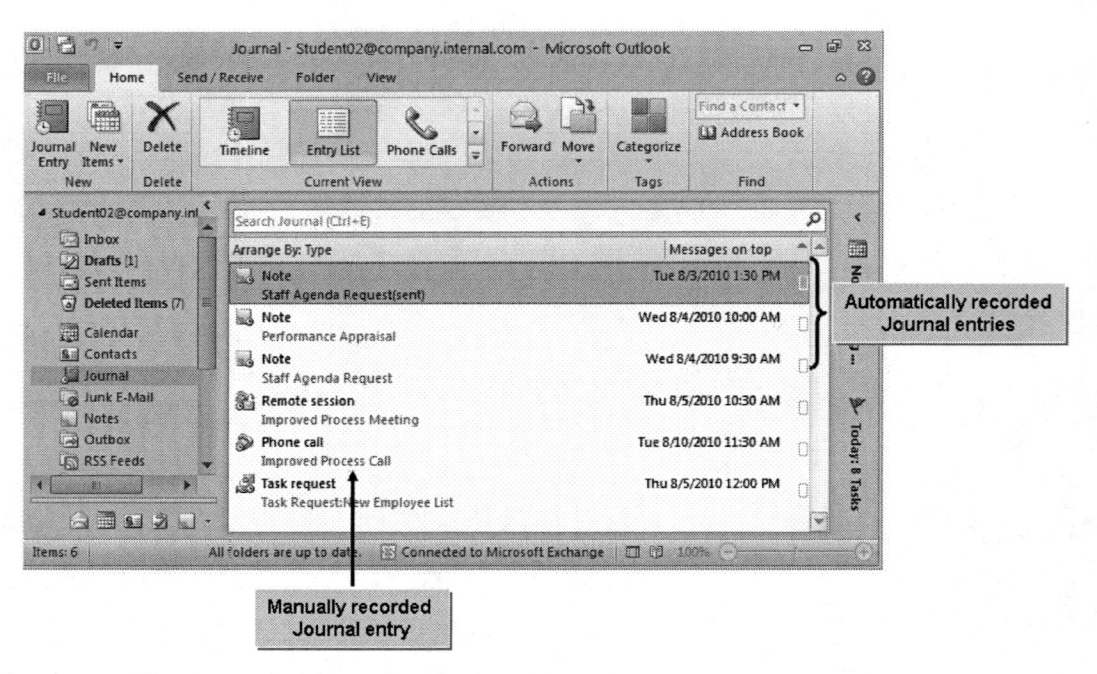

Figure 4-1: The Journal with entries displayed by type.

Lesson 4: Tracking Activities Using the Journal

Journal Views

You can group and arrange your Journal entries by changing the Journal views. There are various types of Journal views.

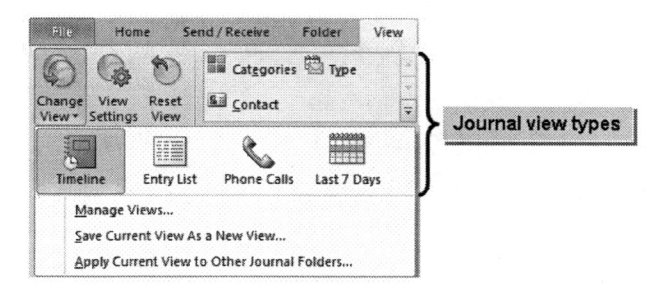

Figure 4-2: The Journal view types.

View	Description
Categories	Displays journal entries from a specified category.
Type	Displays items in a timeline format and groups by entry type. For example, all email messages and all meeting requests are grouped together under respective categories. This is the default view.
Contact	Displays journal entries to and from a particular contact.
Entry List	Displays journal entries in a table, rather than as a timeline.
Phone Calls	Displays all the phone call Journal entries.
Last 7 Days	Displays journal entries made or accessed during the past seven days in a list.

How to Automatically Record a Journal Entry

Procedure Reference: Record a Journal Entry Automatically

To record a journal entry automatically:

1. Display the Folder list.
   - At the bottom of the Quick Launch bar, click the **Folder List** button, or;
   - In the Quick Launch bar, from the **Configure buttons** drop-down list, select **Show More Buttons** twice, and then select the **Folder List** tab.
2. In the Folder list, select the **Journal** folder.
3. In the **Microsoft Outlook** message box, click **Yes** to display the **Journal Options** dialog box.
4. Set the types of activities that you want the Journal to track using the **Journal Options** dialog box.
   - To record items, in the **Automatically record these items** section, check the check boxes for the items that you want recorded.
   - To record items for specific contacts, in the **For these contacts** section, check the check boxes for the contacts you want the items to be recorded for.
   - To record Microsoft program files, in the **Also record files from** section, check the check boxes for programs whose files you want to record.
5. If necessary, in the **Double-clicking a journal entry** section, select your preference.
6. If necessary, click the **AutoArchive Journal Entries** button to open the **Journal Properties** dialog box, to configure archive settings for the Journal folder.
7. Click **OK** to set journal options.
8. The journal will record your Outlook items when work is performed.

Procedure Reference: Open a Journal Entry

To open a Journal entry:

1. Display the Journal folder.
2. Open the journal entry.
   - In the **Journal Options** dialog box, in the **Double-clicking a journal entry** section, select the **Opens the journal entry** option, and double-click the journal entry, or;
   - Right-click the desired journal entry to display the shortcut menu and then choose **Open journal entry.**

> The steps to open the item referred to by a journal entry are the same as those for opening a journal entry, except that you will select your preference based on the **Opens the item referred to by the journal entry** option.

Microsoft® Office Outlook® 2010: Level 2

ACTIVITY 4-1
Recording a Journal Entry Automatically

Scenario:
You need to do a better job of keeping track of how your time is spent, specifically with regard to creating email messages and scheduling meetings with your partners.

---

1. Display the Journal and the **Journal Options** dialog box.

   a. At the bottom of the Quick launch bar, click the **Folder List** button.

   b. In the Folder list, select the **Journal** folder.

   c. In the **Microsoft Outlook** warning box, click **Yes** to display the **Journal Options** dialog box.

2. Set the Journal options to record email messages, and meeting requests for your partner.

   a. In the **Journal Options** dialog box, in the **Automatically record these items** section, check the **E-mail Message** and **Meeting request** check boxes.

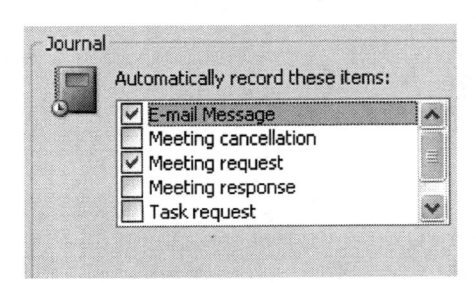

   b. In the **Journal Options** dialog box, in the **For these contacts** section, select your partner.

   c. Click **OK**.

3. **True or False? When you first turn a Journal on, there are Journal entries already recorded in it.**

   ___ True
   ___ False

4. Send an email message to your partner asking for a resume of a potential candidate, and view the recorded Journal Entry form for the sent message.

   a. If necessary, press **F9** to update all Outlook items.

Lesson 4: Tracking Activities Using the Journal   **117**

b. On the **Home** tab, in the **New** group, choose **New Items→E-mail Message** to open a new Message window.

c. Create and send an email message to your partner with the subject **Resume Request** and the message *Do you have the resume for Susan Jones?*

d. Double-click the **Resume Request (sent)** journal entry to open the journal entry form.

> If working in pairs, you might receive both the sent and received **Resume request** journal entries.

e. Close the journal entry form.

> In the **Journal Options** dialog box, in the **Double-clicking a journal entry** section, the **Opens the journal entry** option was set for the **Journal entry**, and not the item referred to in the Journal.

5. From the Journal, review the Resume Request message.

   a. Right-click the **Resume Request** journal entry to display the shortcut menu.

   b. Select the **Open Item Referred To** option to review the message.

   c. Close the Message window.

Microsoft® Office Outlook® 2010: Level 2

TOPIC B
Record a Journal Entry Manually

You have automatically recorded a journal entry. Knowing how to use automatic journaling to track the work that you do is helpful; however, you may have activities that cannot be automatically tracked. In this topic, you will use the journal to manually record a journal entry.

Not all activities can be recorded automatically by the journal. Take, for example, a trip to the office supply store for a printer cartridge, or a call you made from your personal cell phone. Fortunately, the journal allows you to manually enter these types of tasks.

Journal Entry Forms

A **Journal Entry** form is used for manually recording journal entries. There are a variety of entry form options.

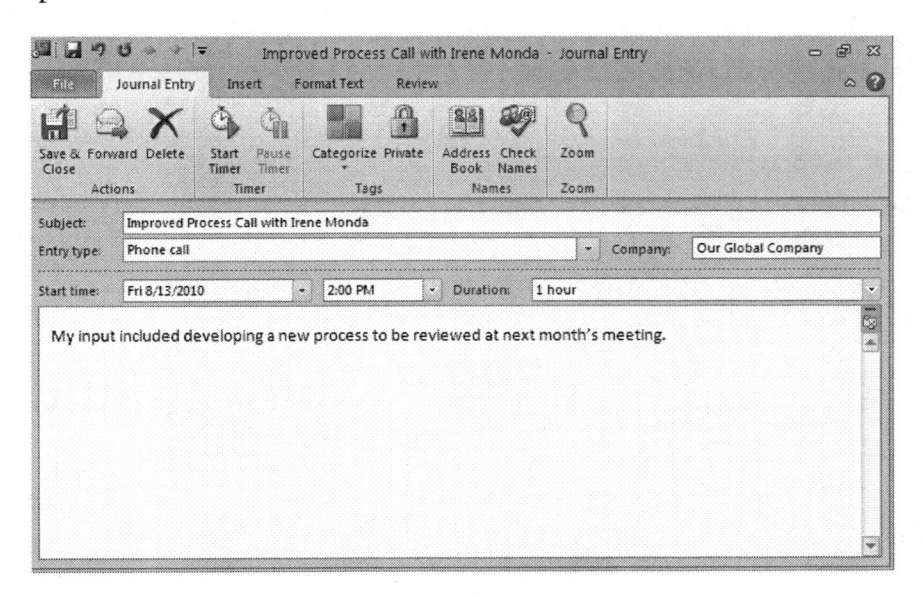

Figure 4-3: A Journal Entry form of the type Phone call.

Option	Description
Subject	Allows you to type a description of the activity.
Entry type	Lists a number of entry types, such as phone calls and meetings, from which to choose.
Company	Allows you to specify the company name.
Start Time	Allows you to specify the time period for a particular activity.
Duration	Allows you to specify the time that you spent on an activity.

Lesson 4: Tracking Activities Using the Journal **119**

How to Manually Record a Journal Entry

Procedure Reference: Record a Journal Entry Manually

To record a Journal entry manually:

1. On the **Home** tab, in the **New** group, click **New Items** and select **More Items→Journal Entry** to display a new Journal Entry form.
2. In the **Subject** text box, type the activity description.
3. From the **Entry Type** drop-down list, select an appropriate entry type for the activity.

> You cannot create your own entry type.

4. Set the other options as required.
   - Enter a company name.
   - Enter a start time or duration.
   - Enter any comments.
   - Mark the item private.
5. Click **OK** to apply the settings.
6. In the **Actions** group, click **Save & Close.**

ACTIVITY 4-2
Recording a Journal Entry Manually

Setup:
The journal is displayed.

Scenario:
You just spent an hour on the telephone with a contact, Irene Monda, and you want this activity tracked in the journal, so that you could efficiently monitor the time spent on that particular conversation

1. Create a new journal entry.

    a. On the **Home** tab, in the **New** group, click **Journal Entry**.

    b. Enter the subject text as *Improved Process Call*

    c. Verify that the **Entry type** is **Phone call**.

    d. From the **Duration** drop-down list, select **1 hour**.

    e. Enter the message text *My input included developing a new process to be reviewed at next month's meeting.*

2. Select the contact Irene Monda as a participant and save the entry.

    a. On the **Journal Entry** tab, in the **Names** group, click **Address Book**.

    b. In the **Select Contacts** dialog box, from the **Items** list, select **Monda, Irene** and click **OK**.

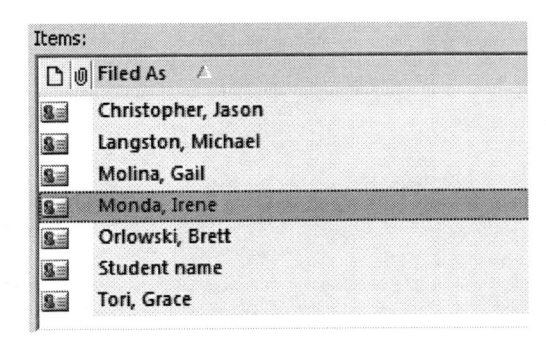

Lesson 4: Tracking Activities Using the Journal 121

Microsoft® Office Outlook® 2010: Level 2

      c.   In the **Actions** group, click **Save & Close.**

3. **What is true about the Improved Process Call Journal entry displayed in the journal?**

    a) It is represented by an icon of a telephone.

    b) It identifies contact information.

    c) It is displayed under an expanded Phone Call entry type.

    d) It displays the duration of the activity.

4. Ensure that the phone call entry type has been assigned to Irene Monda's contact data.

    a.   On the **Home** tab, in the **Current view** group, choose **Phone Calls.**

    b.   Observe that the **Improved Process Call** entry is listed.

    c.   In the **Contact** section, verify that **Irene Monda** is listed.

Lesson 4: Tracking Activities Using the Journal

TOPIC C
Modify a Journal Entry

You have automatically and manually recorded journal entries; however, journal entry information may change. In this topic, you will modify an existing journal entry.

Perhaps you made an error while entering a manual journal entry; you know that it took you three hours to complete a project, but it appears as though it took thirteen minutes. The Outlook journal makes it easy to modify journal entries.

How to Modify a Journal Entry
Procedure Reference: Modify a Journal Entry

To modify a journal entry:

1. With the journal displayed, open the **Journal Entry** form that you need to modify.
2. Replace any information that you want to edit with the correct data.
   a. Open the existing journal entry.
   b. Edit the existing subject to reflect the new one.
   c. From the **Entry type** drop-down list, select the desired entry.
3. Save and close the modified entry.

> To delete a Journal entry, select the entry and press **Delete**.

Procedure Reference: Turn Off Automatic Journaling

To turn off automatic journaling:

1. On the **File** tab, click **Options** to display the **Outlook Options** dialog box.
2. In the **Outlook Options** dialog box, on the **Notes and Journal** tab, click **Journal Options** to display the **Journal Options** dialog box.
3. Uncheck all of the check boxes in the **Automatically record these items** and **Also record files from** sections.
4. Click **OK** twice to close the **Journal Options** and then close the **Outlook Options** dialog boxes.

ACTIVITY 4-3
Modifying a Journal Entry

Scenario:
After some consideration, you decide that the Improved Process Call should have been labeled and tracked as a meeting rather than as a phone call. You also want to view the journal entries in a list that displays duration information.

1. Edit the **Improved Process Phone Call** journal entry so that it appears as a meeting.

    a. With the journal displayed, open the **Improved Process Call** journal entry form.

    b. Edit the subject to read **Improved Process Meeting**

    c. In the **Entry type** drop-down list, scroll up and select **Meeting.**

    d. Save and close the Journal entry.

2. Change the Journal view to Entry List view.

    a. On the **Home** tab, in the **Current View** group, choose **Entry List.**

    b. Observe the **Entry List** view in the **Journal** folder.

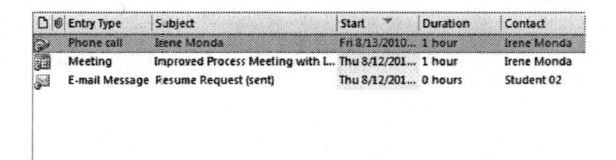

    c. If necessary, you can explore the other views.

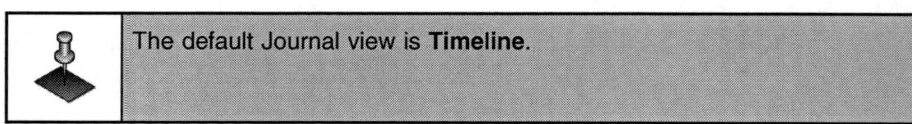

    > The default Journal view is **Timeline**.

3. Turn off the Journal.

    a. On the **File** tab, click **Options** to display the **Outlook Options** dialog box.

    b. In the **Outlook Options** dialog box, click **Notes and Journal** tab, and then click **Journal Options** to display the **Journal Options** dialog box.

c. Uncheck all of the check boxes in the **Automatically record these items** section.

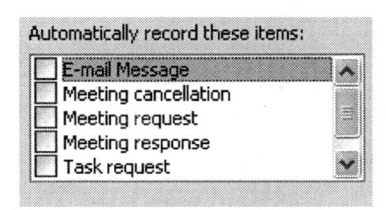

Automatically record these items:
- [ ] E-mail Message
- [ ] Meeting cancellation
- [ ] Meeting request
- [ ] Meeting response
- [ ] Task request

d. Click **OK** twice.

Lesson 4 Follow-up

In this lesson, you tracked activities using the Journal tool. Whether you need to track activities relating to a special project for billing purposes, or track activities that relate to a specific contact, you can use Outlook's Journal to assist you.

1. **What are the advantages of using the journal tool?**

2. **What types of activities would you track using the Outlook Journal?**

5 | Managing Tasks

Lesson Time: 40 minutes

Lesson Objectives:

In this lesson, you will assign and track tasks.

You will:

- Assign a task to another user.
- Reply to a task request.
- Send a task update.
- Track an assigned task.

Introduction

You have used Outlook's Journal to track your work and interactions. You can also keep track of projects that you are working on. In this lesson, you will manage tasks by assigning them to others or by sending information.

Imagine working on a project with an accelerated schedule. In order to complete it on time, you may need to assign project tasks to other coworkers. Once tasks are assigned, Outlook can keep you up-to-date on task progress so that you can ensure timely completion.

TOPIC A
Assign a Task

You manually and automatically entered Journal entries to keep track of your tasks. Apart from creating tasks for yourself, you can assign existing tasks or newly created tasks to others. In this topic, you will assign a task to someone else.

Is your own task list growing faster than you can manage? Maybe it is time to delegate. By formally delegating a task through Outlook, rather than casually asking a coworker, there will not be any question about who is responsible for the task.

The Task Request Form

A *Task Request form* is an Outlook feature used to request updates and status reports on the progress of a task. The Task Request form contains all of the data about the task item, and fields for the start date, due date, status, priority, and % complete. Additional options allow you to keep an updated copy of a task, or check the status of a particular task. These options are enabled by default.

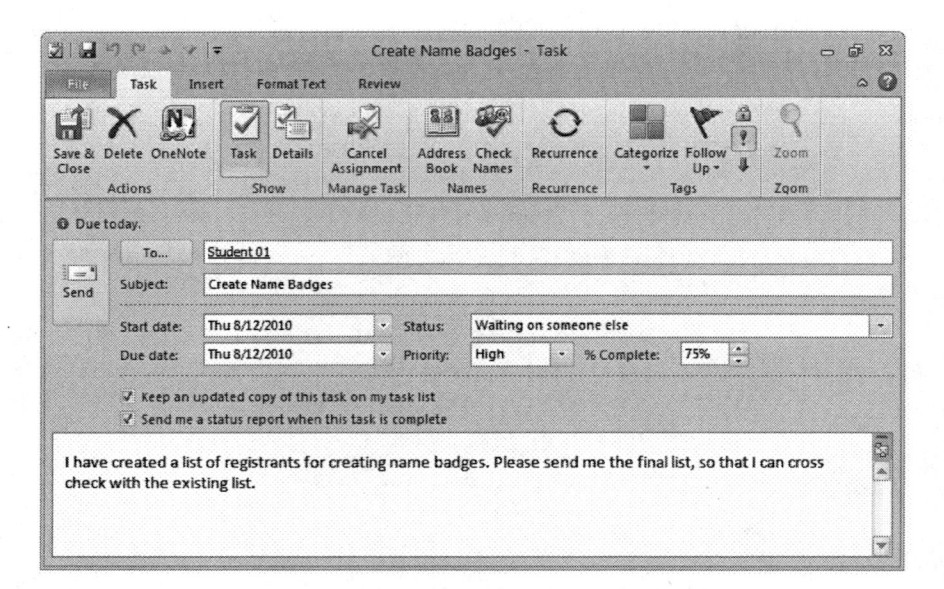

Figure 5-1: The task request form requesting a task to be performed within a day.

> The **To** field in a task request works the same way as the **To** field in an email item. Click the **To** button to open the **Select Task Recipient: Global Address List** dialog box and select a recipient for the task assignment.

Status Options

Outlook provides five status options, each with an associated percent complete value or range.

Status Option	Indicates That the Task
Not Started	Has not yet started. The value in the **% Complete** field is 0.
In Progress	Has already started and is in progress. You can enter the percentage of work that has been completed so far in the **% Complete** field. The value must be in the 1–99 range.
Completed	Has been completed. The value in the **% Complete** field is 100.
Waiting on someone else	Is waiting on someone else. You can enter the percentage of work that has been completed so far in the **% Complete** field. The value must be in the 0–100 range.
Deferred	Has been deferred. You can enter the percentage of work that has been completed so far in the **% Complete** field. The value must be in the 0–100 range.

How to Assign a Task

Procedure Reference: Assign a New Task

To assign a new task:

1. In the Quick launch bar, select the **Tasks** tab.
2. On the **Home** tab, in the **New** group, click **New Items** and select **Task Request** to open a new Task Request form.

> The Task Request form is similar to the Task form, except that it includes a **To** line and a **Send** button.

3. In the **To** text box, enter the user's name to whom you want to assign the task.
4. In the **Subject** text box, enter the task description.
5. In the **Due date** and **Start date** text boxes, enter the desired dates, or click the date picker arrows to select the dates from the calendar.
6. If necessary, from the **Priority** drop-down list, select the desired priority: **Normal, Low,** or **High.**
7. If necessary, type a message in the note area.
8. If necessary, assign a color category to the task.
   a. On the **Task** tab, in the **Tags** group, click **Categorize** and select **All Categories** to easily identify and group the associated items in the task.
   b. In the **Color Categories** dialog box, click **New.**
   c. In the **Add New Category** dialog box, in the **Name** text box, type a color category name.
   d. In the **Color** text box, select a color.
   e. If necessary, select a shortcut key, and click **OK** twice to close the dialog boxes.

9. If you would like to keep an updated copy of the task on your task list or receive a status report when the task is complete, check the appropriate check boxes in the Task form.

> Both of these check boxes in the Task form are selected by default.

10. Click **Send.**
11. If necessary, on the **Task** tab, in the **Tags** group, click **Categorize** and select the existing task.

ACTIVITY 5-1
Assigning Tasks to Others

Scenario:
As project coordinator for an upcoming job expo scheduled for the last Friday of next month, you have tasks that need to be completed. You have determined that the following two tasks can be delegated to a coworker:

- Create Name Badges: Due the day prior to the expo.
- Brochure Layout: Due two weeks from today.

---

1. Create a task request and address it to your partner.

    a. On the Quick launch bar, select the **Tasks** tab.

    b. On the **Home** tab, in the **New** group, click **New Items** and select **Task Request** to open a new Task Request form.

    c. Address the task request to your partner.

    d. In the **Subject** text box, type **Create Name Badges**

---

2. Include the due date information and a note about the participant count.

    a. From the **Due date** drop-down list, select the last Friday of next month.

    b. In the note area, type **Number of participants to follow**

    > Do we have the final list yet?
    >
    > Please send me a purchase order
    > ------------
    > Number of participants to follow

3. Assign the task to a new color category named **Job Expo** and send the message.

   a. On the **Task** tab, in the **Tags** group, click **Categorize** and select **All Categories.**

   b. In the **Color Categories** dialog box, click **New.**

   c. In the **Add New Category** dialog box, in the **Name** text box, type **Job Expo** to assign a name for the new color category.

   d. In the **Color** text box, select the desired color and click **OK.**

   > In the **Add New Category** dialog box, choosing a shortcut key is optional.

   e. In the **Color Categories** dialog box, click **OK.**

   f. In the Task form, click **Send.**

   g. Observe that a color category appears for the assigned task.

4. Create a request for the Brochure Layout task.

   a. On the **Home** tab, in the **New** group, select **New Items→Task Request** to open a new Task Request form.

   b. Address it to your partner.

   c. Enter the subject text as **Brochure Layout**

   d. From the **Due date** drop-down list, select a due date of two weeks from today.

   e. On the **Task** tab, in the **Tags** group, click **Categorize** and select **Job Expo** to assign the task to the Job Expo category.

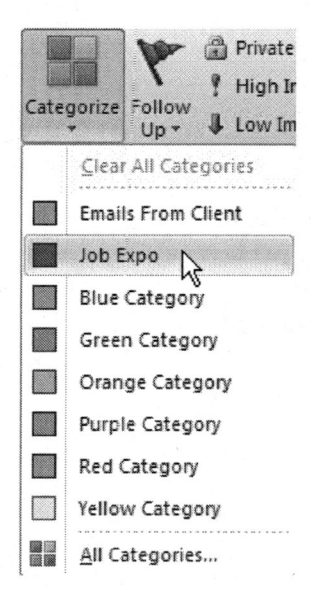

f. Send the task request.

g. If necessary, press **F9** to update all Outlook items.

TOPIC B
Reply to a Task Request

You assigned a task to another user by sending out a task request. There may be instances when you are assigned a task and have to forward periodic updates about the task to the person who assigned the task to you. In this topic, you will reply to a task.

Once a task is assigned to you, you will need to decide whether or not you want to acknowledge task responsibility. Outlook offers different reply options for a task request. Understanding these options and their implications is important in communicating tasks' responsibility.

Reply Options

Outlook offers three options for replying to a task request. Each option functions differently when a user accepts the task, rejects the task, or assigns the task to someone else.

Figure 5-2: The reply options on the Task tab.

Reply Option	Description
Accept	• A message is sent to the person who assigned the task, notifying him or her that the task was accepted.
	• You become the new owner of the task. You are the only one who can modify task information.
	• The task request is moved from your Inbox to your Tasks folder.
	• You may be expected to send updates about task progress to the person who assigned the task, if this was specified in the request.
Decline	• The task request is returned to the person who sent it.
	• The task request message is deleted from your Inbox.
Assign Task	• The task is assigned to another person.
	• The new assignee becomes the owner of the task.

How to Reply to a Task Request

Procedure Reference: Reply to a Task Request

To reply to a task request:

1. Display the contents of the task request.
   - In the Inbox, open the task request message, or;
   - Select the task request message, and view the message in the Reading pane.
2. Reply to the task request.
   - On the **Task** tab, in the **Respond** group, click **Accept** to accept the task with comments.
     a. In the **Accepting Task** warning box, select the **Edit the response before sending** option.
     b. Click **OK.** A Message window is displayed.
     c. In the Message window, type your comments.
   - On the **Task** tab, in the **Respond** group, click **Decline** to decline the task with comments.
     a. In the **Declining Task** warning box, select **Edit the response before sending** and click **OK** to send the response.
     b. A new Task form is displayed and the InfoBar states that you have declined this task.
     c. In the Message window, type your comments.

   > You can also accept or decline a task using the **Accept** or **Decline** button, respectively, in the Reading pane, instead of opening the task request message.

3. Click **Send** to send the reply.
4. If necessary, determine whether you are expected to send periodic task updates, and then send your reply.
   a. On the **Task** tab, in the **Show** group, click **Details.**
   b. Observe that the originator's user name is displayed in the **Update list** text box, indicating that updates will be sent to this user. On the **Task** tab, in the **Show** group, click **Task** to return to the message.
   c. In the Task form, click **Send.**
5. If necessary, read the accepted task message.
   a. Open the **Task Accepted** message.
   b. Observe the message displayed in the InfoBar, indicating that the other person has accepted this task and close the message.
6. If necessary, reclaim ownership of a declined task.
   a. Open the **Task Declined** message.
   b. On the **Task** tab, in the **Manage Task** group, click **Return To Task List** and observe the due date that appears in the InfoBar.
   c. Close the message.

Microsoft® Office Outlook® 2010: Level 2

ACTIVITY 5-2
Replying to a Task Request

Scenario:
You have received two task requests, and based on their due dates and your current workload, you need to accept the Create Name Badge task and decline the Brochure Layout task. You also need to request a purchase order from the task originator and inquire about when she expects to receive updates about the task.

1. Accept the Create Name Badges task request and include a note in the message requesting authorization to purchase name badges.

   a. Display the **Client X** folder.

   b. Open the **Task Request: Create Name Badges** message.

   c. Observe that the assignment information about the task appears on the InfoBar.

   d. On the **Task** tab, in the **Respond** group, click **Accept**.

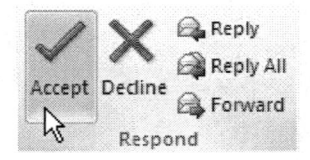

   e. In the **Accepting Task** warning box, select the **Edit the response before sending** option and click **OK**.

136 Lesson 5: Managing Tasks

f. A Task form addressed to your partner is displayed. The InfoBar states that you have accepted this task. In the message body, type **Please send me a purchase order**

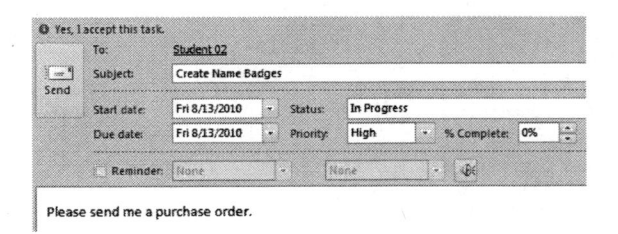

2. Determine whether you are expected to send periodic updates about this task and then send your reply.

   a. On the **Task** tab, in the **Show** group, click **Details.**

   b. Observe that your partner's user name is displayed in the **Update List** section, indicating that updates will be sent to this user.

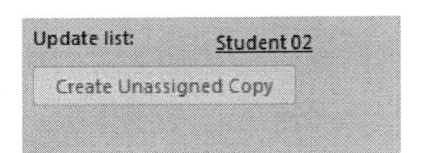

   c. On the **Task** tab, in the **Show** group, click **Task** to return to the message.

   d. In the Task form, click **Send.**

3. Decline the task request titled Brochure Layout.

   a. In the Inbox folder, open the **Task Request: Brochure Layout** message.

   b. On the **Task** tab, in the **Respond** group, click **Decline.**

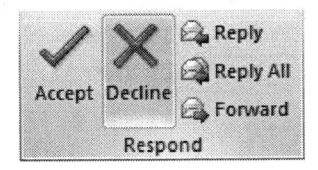

Lesson 5: Managing Tasks

c. In the **Declining Task** warning box, select the **Edit The Response Before Sending** option and click **OK** to send the response.

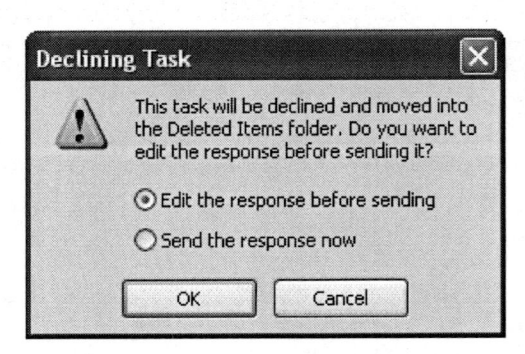

d. A Task form, addressed to your partner, is displayed. The InfoBar states that you have declined this task. In the message body, type *I can not accept this task due to prior project commitments.*

e. Click **Send**.

f. If necessary, press **F9** to update all Outlook items.

g. Display the **Sent Items** folder.

h. Observe that two new messages, **Task Declined** and **Task Accepted**, are displayed.

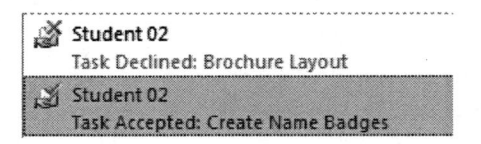

4. Read the accepted task message.

   a. Select the **Client X** folder.

   b. Open the **Task Accepted: Create Name Badges** message.

   c. Observe that a message is displayed in the InfoBar indicating that your partner accepted this task.

   d. Close the message.

   > Closing the message automatically replaces the task in your Tasks folder with the task update.

5. Reclaim ownership of the declined task.

   a. Open the **Task Declined: Brochure Layout** message.

   b. On the **Task** tab, in the **Manage Task** group, click **Return to Task List**.

   c. Observe that the due date appears in the InfoBar.

   d. Close the message.

TOPIC C
Send a Task Update

You have delegated a task to someone else, as well as accepted a task request that another user assigned to you. You may need to send regular updates on the progress of the tasks assigned to you. In this topic, you will send an update for a task that you have accepted.

Because it is important to communicate task progress, once you have accepted responsibility for tasks, you do not want to keep the task originator in the dark regarding your progress, or any obstacles preventing progress. By sending a status report to the task originator which details how much of each task you have completed, the originator can determine whether additional support is needed.

Status Reports

The status report is a detailed email that contains details such as the **Status, % complete,** and **Actual work** hours spent on the task. The *Send Status Report* button enables you to send an email detailing the status of a specific task. This button is displayed only for an existing task.

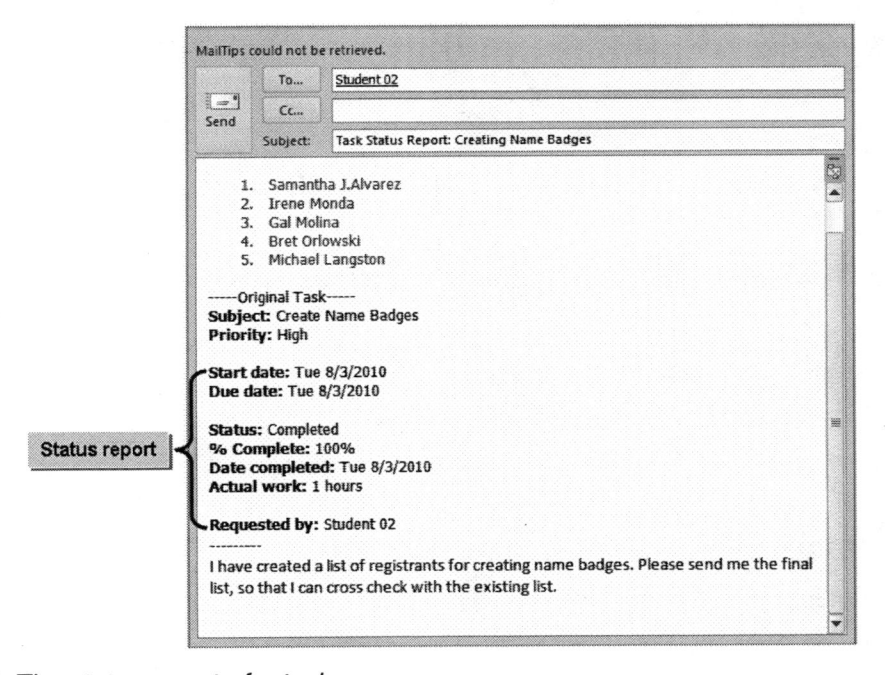

Figure 5-3: The status report of a task.

The Update List

On the **Task** tab, in the **Show** group, click **Details** to view the details about who will receive updates to this task. The **Update list** text box displays user names of those who will receive updates.

How to Send a Task Update

Procedure Reference: Update Task Information and Send a Task Update

To update task information and send a task update:

1. Open the task that you want to update.
2. In the Task form, enter the updated information. Any previously entered information can be modified, and new information added.
   - From the **Status** drop-down list, select the desired status: **Not Started**, **In Progress**, **Completed**, **Waiting On Someone Else**, or **Deferred**.
   - From the **Priority** drop-down list, select the desired priority: **Low**, **Normal**, or **High**.
   - In the **% Complete** text box, type a percentage.
   - If necessary, in the message body, type a message.

   > On the **Task** tab, in the **Show** group, click **Details** to view the details of who will receive updates to this task. The **Update List** text box displays user names of those who will receive updates.

3. Send the status report.
   a. On the **Task** tab, in the **Manage Task** group, click **Send Status Report**.
   b. If necessary, in the message body, type a status message.
   c. Click **Send** to send the status report.
4. On the **Task** tab, in the **Actions** group, click **Save & Close**. A task update is automatically sent to everyone on the update list.

Procedure Reference: Mark the Status of a Task as Deferred

To mark the status of a task as deferred:

1. Open the task that you want to update.
2. In the Task form, enter the updated information.
   - From the **Status** drop-down list, select **Deferred**.
   - From the **Priority** drop-down list, select the desired priority: **Low**, **Normal**, or **High**.
   - In the **% Complete** text box, type a percentage.
   - If necessary, in the message body, type a message.
3. Send the status report.

Procedure Reference: Modify Task Options

To modify task options:

1. On the **File** tab, click **Options** to display the **Outlook Options** dialog box.
2. On the **Task** tab, in the **Task options** section, modify task options.
3. If necessary, click **OK** to close any open dialog boxes.

Task Options

Task options include coloring overdue tasks, coloring completed tasks, keeping updated copies of assigned tasks on the **My Tasks** list, sending status reports when assigned tasks are completed, and setting reminders on tasks with due dates. For example, you can modify overdue tasks to appear in a color other than the default red.

ACTIVITY 5-3
Sending a Task Update

Scenario:
Your manager expects weekly reports on the status of tasks she assigns. You have completed half of the Create Name Badges task, but are waiting to receive the final list of registrants. You need to update her on the priority and status of this task and then send the status report.

Student 02

1. Update the task information.

    a. Select the **Tasks** tab.

    b. In the Tasks list, open the **Create Name Badges** task.

    c. From the **Status** drop-down list, select **In Progress.**

    d. From the **Priority** drop-down list, select **High.**

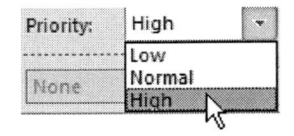

    e. In the **% Complete** text box, type *50%*

    f. In the message body, before the original message, type *Do we have the final list yet?*

    g. Press **Enter** twice.

2. Send the status report.

    a. On the **Task** tab, in the **Manage Task** group, click **Send Status Report.**

    b. In the message body, type *Task in progress* and click **Send** to send the status report to your partner.

    c. On the **Task** tab, in the **Actions** group, click **Save & Close** to send the update to your partner.

Lesson 5: Managing Tasks 141

TOPIC D
Track Assigned Tasks

You have sent updates for the tasks you accepted. There will also be instances when you create task requests. And, you may want to receive periodic updates and notifications about the assigned task. In this topic, you will track the tasks you have assigned to others.

You have delegated a task and it is your responsibility to track the task that you have assigned. You may want to keep track of who you assigned the task to and the progress being made on the task.

How to Track Assigned Tasks

Procedure Reference: Track Assigned Tasks

To track assigned tasks:

1. Verify the updated task.
    a. On the Quick launch bar, select the **Tasks** tab.
    b. Open the task. The task contains the updated information.
    c. Close the Task form.
2. If necessary, verify the status report.
    a. Display the **Inbox** folder.
    b. Open the status report message. The detailed status of the task is displayed in the message.
    c. Close the message.
3. On the **View** tab, in the **Current View** group, click **Change View** and select **Assigned**.
4. Double-click the task that you wish to track. The InfoBar shows the due date of the last update for this task. The information in the Task form reflects this update.

> In the Task form, on the **Task** tab, in the **Show** group, click **Details** for additional information about the task.

Procedure Reference: Share Task Information with Other Users

To share task information with other users:

1. On the Quick Launch bar, select the **Tasks** tab.
2. Right-click the task message and choose **Forward.** A new Message window opens. The task is inserted as an attachment and the task name displayed in the Subject line.
3. Send the message.

ACTIVITY 5-4
Tracking Assigned Tasks

Scenario:
As project coordinator for the job expo, you need to follow up on the Create Name Badges task in order to track its status.

1. Verify that the task and the status report have been updated.

    a. Select the **Tasks** tab.

    b. Open the **Create Name Badges** task.

    c. Observe that the task contains the updated information.

    d. Close the Task form.

    e. Display the **Client X** folder.

    f. Open the **Task Status Report: Create Name Badges** message.

    g. Observe that the detailed status of the task is displayed in the message.

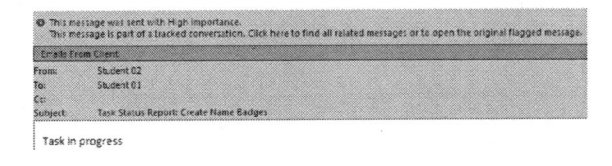

    h. Close the Message window.

2. Display a list of tasks based on priority.

    a. On the Quick launch bar, select the **Tasks** tab.

    b. On the **View** tab, in the **Current View** group, click **Change View** and select **Prioritized**.

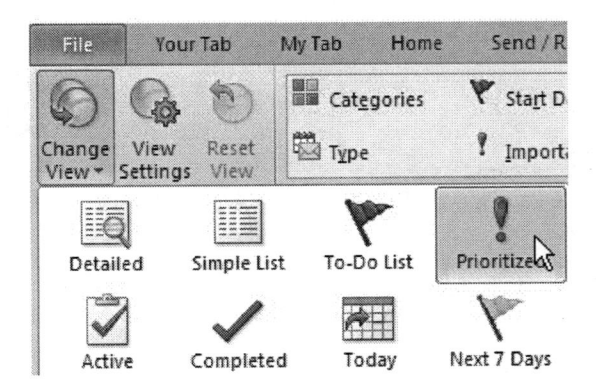

Lesson 5: Managing Tasks 143

c. Observe that the task you have assigned is displayed.

Lesson 5 Follow-up

In this lesson, you assigned tasks to others, as well as accepted, declined, or reassigned those tasks assigned to you. Being able to track the progress of tasks makes even complex projects and demanding deadlines manageable.

1. **When would you assign tasks to a coworker?**

2. **Why is it important to track tasks that have been assigned to coworkers?**

6 Sharing Folder Information

Lesson Time: 40 minutes

Lesson Objectives:

In this lesson, you will share folder information.

You will:
- Specify folder permissions.
- Access another user's folder.
- Send calendar information in an email message.
- Delegate access to a folder.

Introduction

As an Outlook user, you know that assigning and tracking tasks will help keep your work schedule up-to-date. Because Outlook folders contain a wealth of information, it is likely that you will want to share them with others. In this lesson, you will share folder information.

Because good communication can foster successful teamwork, you may want to share the information in your Outlook folders with other people. With Outlook, you can grant varying levels of access to folders and control what other users are able to do within a folder.

TOPIC A
Specify Folder Permissions

You have updated your tasks and tracked the tasks you assigned to others. By default, you are the only user with access to all of your Outlook folders. However, there may be times when you want to share the contents of a folder with your coworkers. In this topic, you will give other users permission to view specific folders.

You would like to give coworkers access to some of your Outlook folders, but you are worried that they may inadvertently modify or delete data. With Outlook, you can control the type of access users have by granting them the appropriate level of access, for example, the ability to read, write, or delete folder items.

Permission Roles

A *permission role* specifies the level of access that another person can have to one of your Outlook folders. The permission role can be modified only by an Outlook user with the owner permission role.

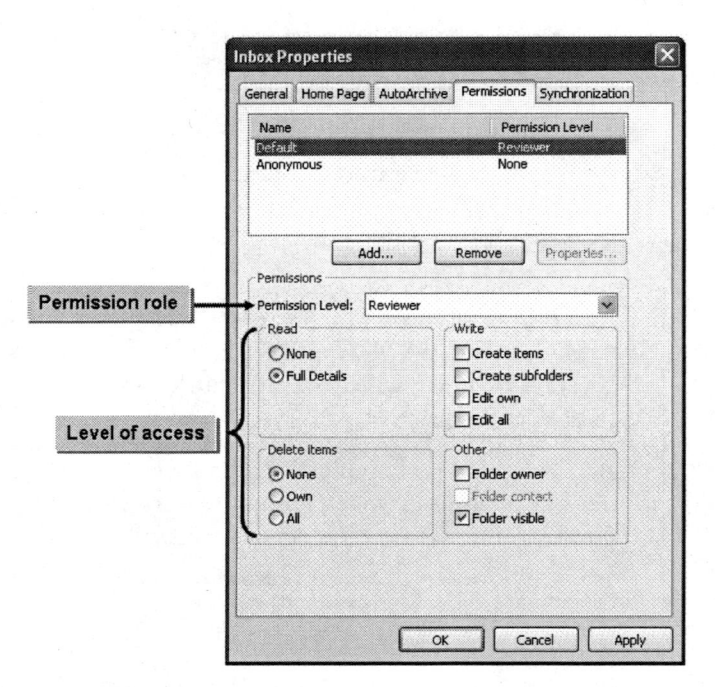

Figure 6-1: The Inbox Properties dialog box displaying the permission roles and levels.

Roles and Their Associated Permission Levels
The available permission roles and their default permission levels are listed in the table.

Items and Files

Role	Read	Create	Modify	Delete	Create Subfolders	Change folder permission levels
Owner	yes	yes	yes	yes	yes	yes
Publishing Editor	yes	yes	yes	yes	yes	no
Editor	yes	yes	yes	yes	no	no
Publishing Author	yes	yes	your own only	your own only	yes	no
Author	yes	yes	your own only	your own only	no	no
Nonediting Author	yes	yes	no	no	no	no
Reviewer	yes	no	no	no	no	no
Contributor	no	yes	no	no	no	no
None	no	no	no	no	no	no
Custom			specified by owner			

Outlook Folders

Outlook folders are useful for helping you manage information, such as creating tasks, appointments, meetings, and contacts, and organizing email.

By default, some of the folders such as **Calendar, Contacts,** and **Tasks,** are displayed as tabs. To display the tabbed items as regular folders, click the **Folder List** button on the Navigation pane. Outlook includes several default folders.

Folder	Description
Inbox	Consists of email messages that you receive from other users.
Outbox	Contains outgoing messages that are waiting to be sent.
Sent Items	Contains messages you have sent to other users.
Drafts	Consists of email messages that you created and saved but have not sent. You can retrieve the messages from the Drafts folder and send them to the desired recipients.
Deleted Items	Contains deleted Outlook items like email, tasks, and contacts. The deleted Outlook items can be restored, if necessary.

Folder	Description
Junk E-mail	Consists of messages that are marked junk. Messages that are not marked junk are moved to the Inbox or to the folder in which they were stored.
Calendar	Contains appointments, reminders, meetings, and tasks that are self-assigned or that are assigned to you by others.
Notes	Provides you with the ability to electronically store your thoughts and ideas as notes. You can easily refer to or update these notes whenever needed.
Contacts	Contains names, addresses, and phone numbers of important personal or business contacts. You also have options to add, sort, and find a contact.
Tasks	Contains an electronic list of what task you need to do and when you need to do it. You can create a task for yourself as well as assign tasks to others.
Journal	Tracks Outlook items that are sent or received from others and displays them in a timeline format.
Search Folders	Displays email messages and other Outlook items based on search criteria. There are three default search folders that can be modified or deleted: • **Categorized Mail**: Any email item with a flag appears in the Categorized Mail search folder. • **Large Mail**: Email items that are larger than 100 kilobytes (KB) appear in the Large Mail search folder. • **Unread Mail**: All unread email items appear in the Unread Mail search folder.
RSS Feeds	This folder displays email from Internet subscribers. When you subscribe to an RSS feed, they appear in the **RSS Feeds** folder in your email folders by default.
Sync Issues	This folder contains all of the synchronization logs.

How to Specify Folder Permissions

Procedure Reference: Specify Default Folder Permissions

To specify default folder permissions:

1. Right-click the folder, choose **Properties,** and then select the **Permissions** tab to display the permissions of that folder.
2. If necessary, from the **Name** list, select **Default.**
3. From the **Permission Level** drop-down list, select a permission level.

> The permissions associated with each level are displayed in the options and check boxes below the **Permission Level** drop-down list.

4. Click **OK** to apply the permissions and close the dialog box.

ACTIVITY 6-1
Specifying Default Calendar Permissions

Setup:
The Tasks folder is displayed.

Scenario:
It is important for all your coworkers to know your work schedule so that they can plan for the meetings that include your presence. Therefore, you want all users to be able to view items in your calendar but not to add, delete, or modify existing items.

1. Set the default permission level to **Reviewer.**

    a. On the Quick launch bar, select the **Calendar** tab and, under **My Calendars**, right-click **Calendar.**

    b. Choose **Properties** to open the **Calendar Properties** dialog box.

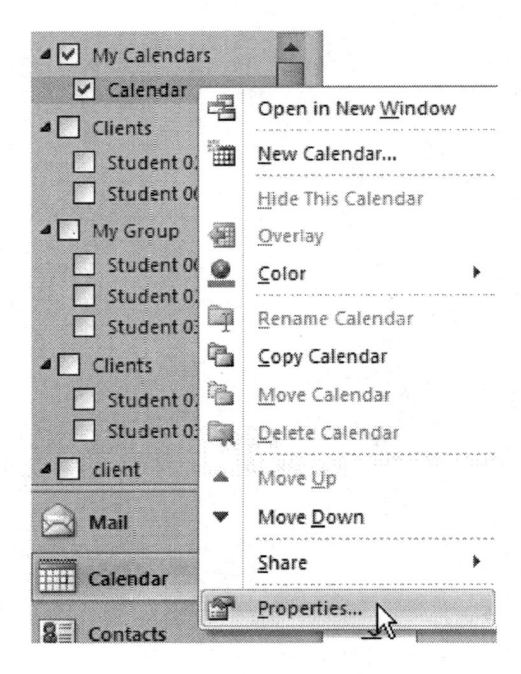

    c.

On the **Permissions** tab, in the **Permissions** section, from the **Permission Level** drop-down list, select **Reviewer.**

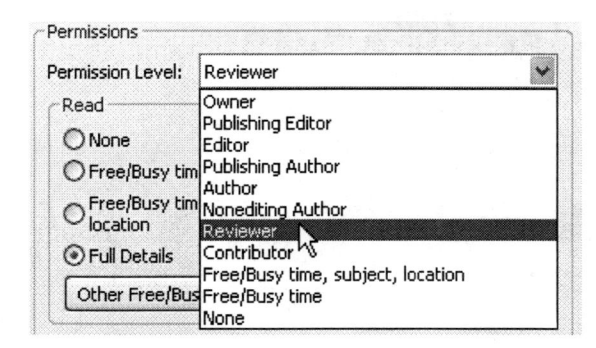

d. Observe that the permissions associated with the Reviewer level are displayed in the options and check boxes in the panel. Click **OK** to apply the permissions and to close the dialog box.

2. **When granting permissions to your Inbox, you must:**

   a) Set a delegate name

   b) Assign permission roles

   c) Assign level of access

   d) Deny permission roles

TOPIC B
Access Another User's Folder

You have given other users access to some of your folders. You may now want to look up the information in your colleague's calendar to coordinate with him. In this topic, you will access and view another Outlook user's calendar.

Given the appropriate access, you may need to view the contents of another Outlook person's folder. Having been given the permission to do so, you can view folders and edit content based upon the permissions assigned to you.

Overlay Mode

Outlook 2010 provides you with the option to view multiple calendars all at once. With the **Overlay** mode on, you can stack calendars one on top of the other. Calendars can include your default Outlook calendars, shared calendars, Internet calendars, or Internet calendar subscriptions. The Overlay mode is useful for finding the free and busy time of others, and for viewing any meeting requests they have accepted or saved. However, before you can access another user's calendar information, you must first have the necessary permission.

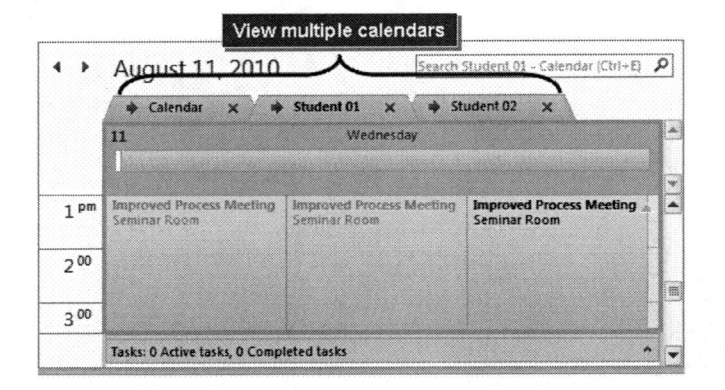

Figure 6-2: A view of different calendars in the Overlay mode.

How to Access Another User's Folder

Procedure Reference: Access Another User's Folder

To access another user's folder:

1. Set the default folder permission levels by right clicking the folder on the Navigation pane and choosing **Properties.**
   - Set the permission level for your Outlook folder.
   - Set the same permission level for the other user's folder for which you have permission, and with whom you want to share your folder information.

   > Permission has to be set independently by the respective Outlook users. If you are having trouble accessing a user's folder, check with the other user to make sure that you have been granted the necessary permission.

2. On the **File** tab, click **Open** and then click **Other User's Folder** to display the **Open Other User's Folder** dialog box.
3. In the **Name** text box, enter the name of the user whose folder you need to access.
   - Type the name or;
   - Click the **Name** button, select the name from the **Global address list** and then click **OK** or;
   - Click the **Name** button, and then double-click the user name.
4. From the **Folder type** drop-down list, select the folder you need to view.
5. Click **OK.**

   > To turn off the display of the other user's folder, uncheck the appropriate check box in the Navigation pane.

Procedure Reference: View Calendars in Overlay Mode

To view calendars in Overlay mode:

1. In the Navigation pane, under **Shared Calendars,** right-click the other user's name and choose **Overlay** to view the calendar in Overlay mode.
2. If necessary, right-click the other user's name and click **Overlay** to switch back to the default calendar view.

ACTIVITY 6-2
Accessing Another User's Calendar Folder

Setup:
The calendar is displayed. The default permission level for your partner's calendar and your calendar is set to Reviewer.

Scenario:
One of your clients wants to know if you and your partner are free to visit his office the following Thursday afternoon from 1:00 to 4:00 PM. So, you need to quickly check your and your partner's calendars.

1. Display your partner's calendar.

    a. On the **File** tab, then click **Open** and click **Other User's Folder.**

    b. In the **Open Other User's Folder** dialog box, click **Name.**

    c. In the **Select Name: Global Address List** dialog box, in the **Name** list, double-click your partner's name.

    d. With Calendar selected in the **Folder type** drop-down list, click **OK** to close the dialog box and to display your partner's calendar.

2. View the calendars in Overlay mode.

    a. In the Navigation pane, uncheck the **Project Leads** check box to hide the calendar group.

    b. In the Navigation pane, under **Shared Calendars,** right-click your partner's name and choose **Overlay** to view the calendars in the Overlay mode.

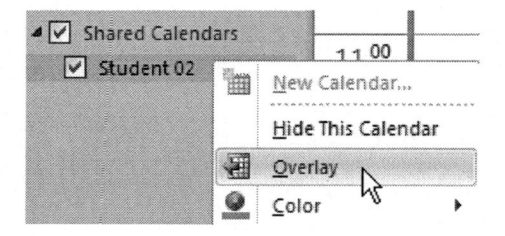

c. Observe that the calendars are displayed in Overlay mode.

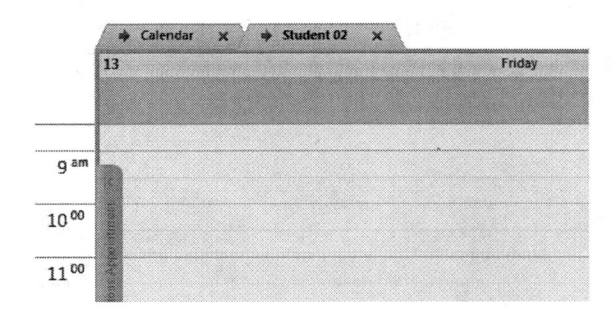

d. In the Navigation pane, under **Shared Calendars,** right-click your partner's name and choose **Overlay** to switch back to the default calendar view.

3. **True or False? In the Side-By-Side mode, your partner's calendar is displayed beside your calendar and a new check box for displaying or hiding the shared calendar is displayed in the Navigation pane.**

    ___ True

    ___ False

4. Check both calendars for availability.

    a. In the date navigator, select next Thursday.

    b. Observe that the selected date is displayed in both calendars.

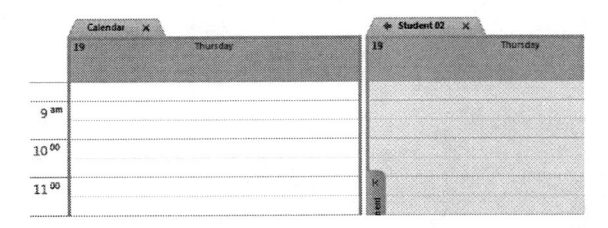

    c. If necessary, scroll down to verify that the 1:00 PM–4:00 PM time slot is available.

5. Hide your partner's calendar.

    a. In the Navigation pane, under **Shared Calendars,** uncheck your partner's check box.

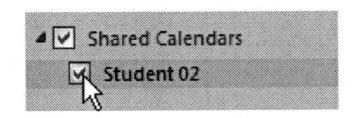

    b. Observe that your partner's calendar is not displayed.

Lesson 6: Sharing Folder Information   157

TOPIC C

Send Calendar Information in an Email Message

You accessed and viewed another user's calendar using Outlook. You may now want to share your calendar information with users who do not have Outlook. In this topic, you will send calendar information through email.

There may be situations where you want to share your calendar information with people who do not have Outlook. You may also send your weekly, monthly or even yearly appointments, events, and meetings schedule to any desired email addresses. In such situations, you can send a snapshot of your calendar through email.

The Send a Calendar via E-mail Dialog Box

The **Send a Calendar via E-mail** dialog box allows you to send calendars to other users in an email message. The dialog box contains options that let you set the date range, working hours, time availability, and the free and busy information.

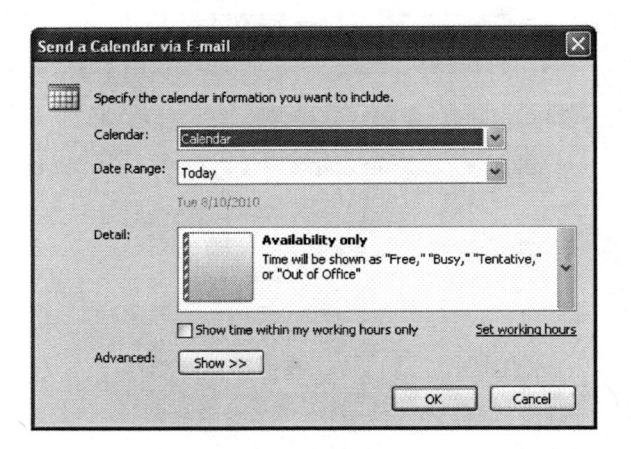

Figure 6-3: The various options in the Send a Calendar Via E-mail dialog box.

Option	Lists
Calendar	The different types of calendars you can choose.
Date Range	A range of dates.
Detail	The options to set the details that the calendar can display. The options are: • **Availability only:** Shows the availability details to confirm if you are free, busy, or out of office. • **Limited details:** Limits details to availability and subjects of calendar items. • **Full details:** Shows the availability and full details of calendar items.

Option	Lists
Show time within my working hours only	Options to set time within your working hours, change planner options, add holidays, and propose new meeting times.
Advanced	Options to mark items private, include attachments, and set email layouts.

How to Send Calendar Information in an Email Message

Procedure Reference: Send Calendar Information via Email

To send calendar information in an email message:

1. On the Quick Launch bar, select the **Calendar** tab.
2. On the **Home** tab, in the **Share** group, click **E-mail Calendar**.
3. Specify the calendar information you want to include.
   a. In the **Send a Calendar via E-mail** dialog box, in the **Calendar** text box, verify whether the **Calendar** option is selected.
   b. From the **Date Range** drop-down list, select the desired date range to specify the calendar information: **Today, Tomorrow, Next 7 Days, Next 30 Days, Whole Calendar**, or **Specify Dates**.
   c. From the **Detail** drop-down list, select the desired option to specify the available details of calendar items: **Availability Only, Limited Details**, or **Full Details**.
4. Click **OK** to close the dialog box and attach the calendar information in the message body.
5. Click **Send** to send the message with calendar information to the recipient.

ACTIVITY 6-3
Sending Calendar Information in an Email Message

Setup:
The calendar is displayed.

Scenario:
One of your colleagues who does not have the Outlook feature has asked you to send her your calendar information for the next seven days. She also asks you to include the details of the calendar items. You have decided to send your calendar information via email.

1. Specify the calendar information you want to include.

   a. On the **Home** tab, in the **Share** group, click **E-mail Calendar.**

   b. In the **Send a Calendar via E-mail** dialog box, in the **Calendar** drop-down list, verify that the **Calendar** option is selected.

   c. From the **Date Range** drop-down list, select **Next 7 days** to specify the calendar information for the next seven days.

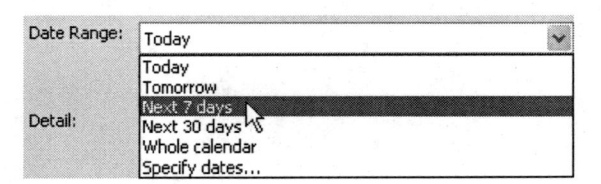

   d. From the **Detail** drop-down list, select **Full details** to specify the full details of calendar items.

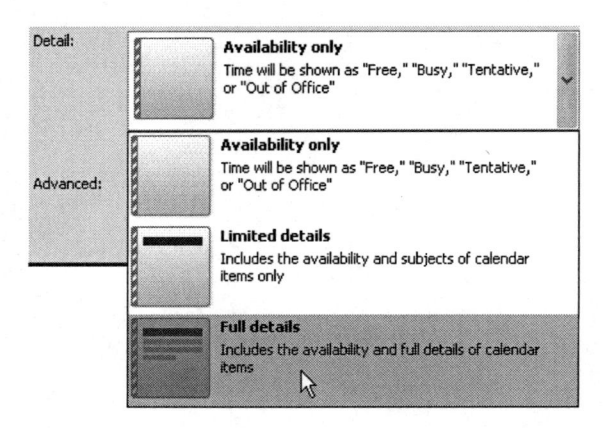

e. Click **OK** to close the dialog box.

f. In the Message window, scroll down to view the **Lunch with Jim** appointment and other calendar details attached in the message body.

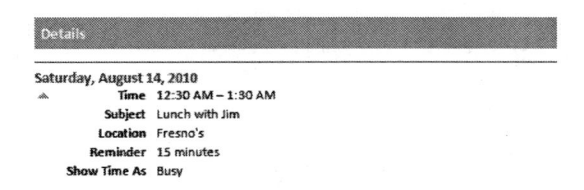

> **Details**
>
> Saturday, August 14, 2010
> Time   12:30 AM – 1:30 AM
> Subject   Lunch with Jim
> Location   Fresno's
> Reminder   15 minutes
> Show Time As   Busy

2. Send the calendar information to your partner.

   a. In the **To** text box, type your partner's name.

   b. In the Message window, click **Send** to send the calendar information.

TOPIC D
Delegate Folder Access to Users

You have sent calendar details through email. There may be situations where you would like to give the Editor access to only one person. In this topic, you will delegate a person to access one of your Outlook folders.

When you assigned default calendar permissions to users, you gave anyone the ability to access the folder. In some cases, this can be dangerous. To get more control over the folders, you can set a delete with required permission levels.

Delegates

A *delegate* is a person who has been given permission to access someone else's Outlook folders. A delegate is assigned one of the same permission roles that can be assigned to a default user; the only difference is that only the specified user, and not all users, is being given access.

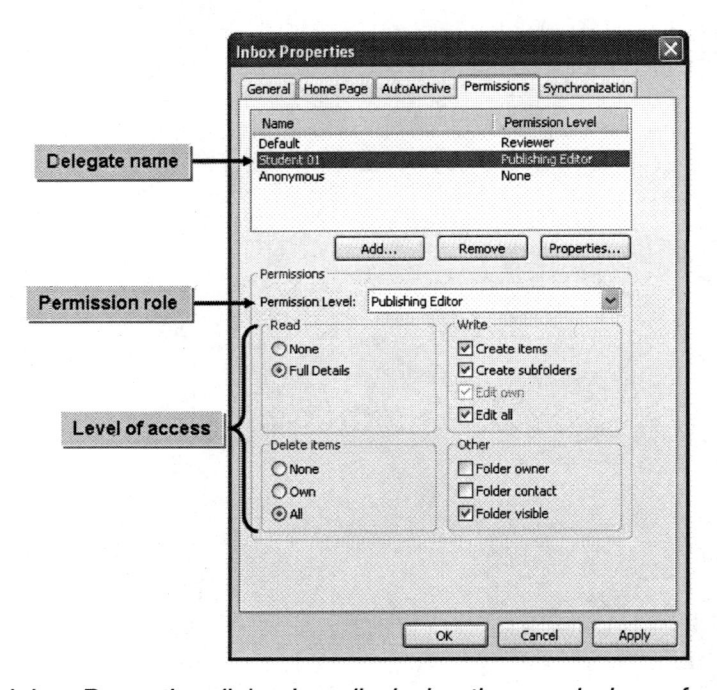

Figure 6-4: The Inbox Properties dialog box displaying the permissions of a delegate.

How to Delegate Access to Folders

Procedure Reference: Delegate Access to a Specific User

To delegate access to a specific user:

1. In the Navigation pane, right-click the desired folder, choose **Properties**, and then select the **Permissions** tab to display the folder's **Permissions** tab.
2. Click **Add** to display the **Add Users** dialog box.
3. In the **Add Users** dialog box, specify the names you want to add.
   - In the **Name** list, double-click the name of the user.
   - In the **Name** list, select the name of the user and click **Add** or;
   - In the **Search** text box, type the name of the user and click **Add.**
4. Click **OK** to add the users to whom you want to delegate access.
5. From the **Permission Level** drop-down list, select a permission level.

> The permissions associated with each level are displayed in the options and check boxes below the **Permission Level** drop-down list.

6. Click **OK** to apply the permissions and close the dialog box.

Procedure Reference: View Items in Another User's Folder

To view items in another user's folder:

1. On the **File** tab, click **Open** and then click **Other User's Folder.**
2. In the **Open Other User's Folder** dialog box, click **Name.**
3. In the **Name** list, double-click the other person's name.
4. Click **OK** to close the dialog box and to display the other person's folder.

Microsoft® Office Outlook® 2010: Level 2

ACTIVITY 6-4
Delegating Your Contacts and the Inbox Folder's Access to Users

Setup:
The calendar is displayed.

Scenario:
You will be out of office for a few days. Because your business contacts list needs to be updated, you have assigned this task to your assistant. He will need access to your Contacts folder to be able to create, edit, and delete any items in that folder. You will also need to delegate Reviewer access to your Inbox folder.

1. Delegate the Contacts folder access to your partner.

    a. On the Quick launch bar, select the **Contacts** tab.

    b. In the Navigation pane, under **My Contacts**, right-click **Contacts** and choose **Properties** to open the **Contacts Properties** dialog box.

    c. In the **Contacts Properties** dialog box, select the **Permissions** tab.

    d. Click **Add** to display the **Add Users** dialog box.

    e. In the **Name** list, double-click your partner's name.

    f. Click **OK.**

Lesson 6: Sharing Folder Information

g. Observe that your partner's name is selected in the **Name** list on the **Permissions** tab.

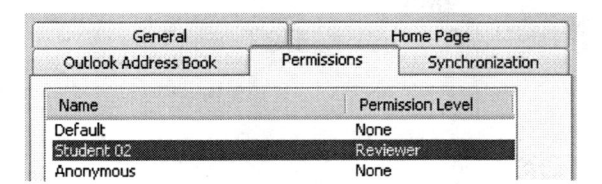

2. Assign Editor permissions.

    a. From the **Permission Level** drop-down list, select **Editor.**

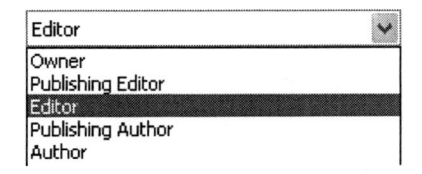

    b. Click **OK** to apply the permissions and close the dialog box.

3. Delegate your Inbox folder access.

    a. Display the **Inbox** folder.

    b. In the Navigation pane, right-click **Inbox,** and choose **Properties.**

    c. In the **Inbox Properties** dialog box, on the **Permissions** tab, click **Add** to display the **Add Users** dialog box.

    d. In the **Name** list, double-click your partner's name and click **OK.**

    e. Observe that your partner's name is selected in the **Name** list on the **Permissions** tab.

4. Assign Reviewer permissions.

    a. From the **Permission Level** drop-down list, select **Reviewer.**

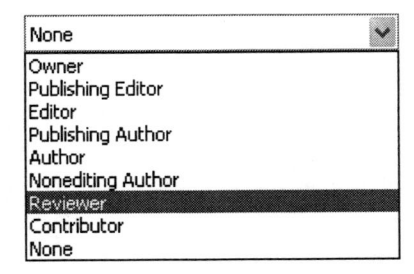

    b. Click **OK** to apply the permissions and close the dialog box.

Lesson 6: Sharing Folder Information   165

ACTIVITY 6-5
Viewing the Messages of Another User's Inbox Folder

Setup:

The Inbox folder is displayed. You have been designated as a delegate for your partner's Inbox folder, with a Reviewer permission level.

Scenario:

As a personal assistant, you have been asked to review the resume of a potential job candidate in your managers Inbox, as your manager is out of office on a vacation and has delegated access of his Inbox to you.

1. Display your partner's Inbox.

    a. On the **File** tab, click **Open** and then click **Other User's Folder**.

    b. In the **Open Other User's Folder** dialog box, click **Name**.

    c. In the **Select Name: Global Address List** dialog box, in the **Name** list, double-click your partner's name.

    d. Click **OK** to close the dialog box and to display your partner's Inbox.

2. Review the message in your partner's Inbox.

    a. Open the **Samantha Alvarez Resume.htm** message.

    b. Verify the qualifications of the candidate.

    c. Close the message.

ACTIVITY 6-6
Viewing and Editing Another User's Contacts

Setup:
The **Contacts** folder is displayed. You have been designated as a delegate for your partner's **Contacts** folder.

Scenario:
Your manager will be out of office and you as his personal assistant, are delegated to view his Contacts folder and to edit a particular contact.

1. Display your partner's Contacts folder.

    a. On the **File** tab, click **Open** and then click **Other User's Folder**.

    b. In the **Open Other User's Folder** dialog box, click **Name**.

    c. In the **Select Name: Global Address List** dialog box, in the **Name** list, double-click your partner's name and click **OK**.

    d. From the **Folder type** drop-down list, choose **Contacts**.

    e. Click **OK** to close the dialog box and to display your partner's Contact folder.

2. Edit Irene Monda's contact form.

    a. Open Irene Monda's contact form.

    b. In the **Job Title** text box, type **CEO** to include a job title.

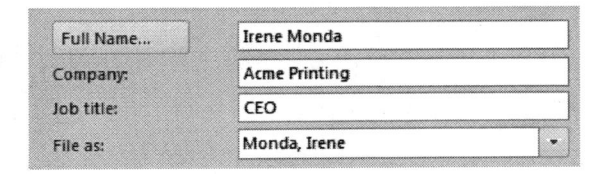

    | Full Name... | Irene Monda |
    | Company: | Acme Printing |
    | Job title: | CEO |
    | File as: | Monda, Irene |

    c. In the **Actions** group, click **Save & Close** to save and close the contact.

3. Verify that the change was made.

    > It may take several minutes for the change to be evident.

    a. On the Quick launch bar, click **Contacts**.

    b. In the Navigation pane, in the **My Contacts** section, select **Contacts**.

c. Open Irene Monda's contact form and observe the changes made in the **Job Title** text box. Save and close the contact.

Lesson 6 Follow-up

In this lesson, you shared your Outlook folder information with other users. You can now open your folders to anyone who wants to use them, specify who will be allowed to access your folders, and set how much—if any—editing they can do. You can also choose to limit access to a specific user or group.

1. **Which of your Outlook folders are you likely to share with other users?**

2. **Who might you assign as a delegate to any of your Outlook folders, and why?**

7 Customizing the Outlook Environment

Lesson Time: 40 minutes

Lesson Objectives:

In this lesson, you will customize the Outlook environment.

You will:

- Customize the ribbon and Quick Access toolbar.
- Customize the To-Do bar.
- Create a folder home page.

Introduction

You have been using Outlook for sometime now and have used many of its commands and tools. Now you may want to organize the Outlook environment in a way that suits your needs and preferences. In this lesson, you will customize the Outlook environment.

At home, you arrange furniture and artwork in a way that reflects your personal style and needs. In a similar way, customizing your work environment ensures that commands are arranged in a way that reflects your needs and work preferences. Organizing commands on your application to suit your preferences ensures that you have easy access to frequently used commands.

TOPIC A
Customize the Ribbon and Quick Access Toolbar

You have worked with various functions in Outlook 2010 and are comfortable, and perhaps proficient, with using the application. You may now want to customize the ribbon and Quick Access toolbar to your liking or workflow, so that you can quickly access many commands that are independent of the currently displayed tab. In this topic, you will customize the ribbon and Quick Access toolbar.

You may have come across many commands that are common to all Outlook items. You had to scan through each item or the ribbon to use a command. This slowed down your working efficiency. Outlook allows you to place these commands on the Quick Access toolbar so you can easily access them whenever you want. You can also customize the ribbon for easy access of commands.

How to Customize the Ribbon and Quick Access Toolbar

Procedure Reference: Customize the Quick Access Toolbar

To customize the Quick Access toolbar:

1. Display the **Outlook Options** dialog box.
2. In the **Outlook Options** dialog box, select **Quick Access Toolbar.**
3. From the **Choose commands from** drop-down list, select a category from which a command needs to be added to the Quick Access toolbar.
4. In the list box below the drop-down list, select a command and click **Add** to add the command to the Quick Access toolbar.
5. If necessary, add more commands to the Quick Access toolbar.
6. If necessary, in the **Customize Quick Access Toolbar** list box, select a command and click **Remove** to remove the command from the Quick Access toolbar.
7. Click **OK** to close the **Outlook Options** dialog box.
8. If necessary, on the ribbon, select a tab, right-click the name of a group, and choose **Add to Quick Access Toolbar** to add the group to the Quick Access toolbar.
9. If necessary, add a command button from the ribbon to the Quick Access toolbar.
   a. On the ribbon, select the tab that has the desired command.
   b. Right-click the command and choose **Add to Quick Access Toolbar.**

> You can add any number of groups to the Quick Access toolbar. However, the ribbon itself cannot be added to the Quick Access toolbar.

Procedure Reference: Reposition the Quick Access Toolbar

To reposition the Quick Access toolbar:

1. Display the **Outlook Options** dialog box.

2. In the **Outlook Options** dialog box, select **Quick Access Toolbar.**
3. Check or uncheck the **Show Quick Access Toolbar below the Ribbon** check box to place the Quick Access toolbar below or above the ribbon.
4. From the **Customize Quick Access Toolbar** drop-down list, select **Show Below The Ribbon** to reposition the Quick Access toolbar below the ribbon.
5. Click **OK** to close the **Outlook Options** dialog box.

Procedure Reference: Delete a Command from the Quick Access Toolbar

To delete a command from the Quick Access toolbar:

1. Display the **Outlook Options** dialog box.
2. In the **Outlook Options** dialog box, select the **Quick Access Toolbar.**
3. Delete a command from the list of commands displayed on the Quick Access toolbar.
   - In the **Outlook Options** dialog box, from the **Customize Quick Access Toolbar** list, select the command to delete, click **Remove,** and then click **OK,** or;
   - On the Quick Access toolbar, right-click the command to delete it and choose **Remove from Quick Access Toolbar.**

Procedure Reference: Customize the Ribbon

To customize the ribbon:

1. Display the **Outlook Options** dialog box.
2. In the **Outlook Options** dialog box, select the **Customize Ribbon** tab.
3. Below the **Customize the Ribbon** list box, click **New Tab** to create a new Ribbon tab.
4. Below the **Customize the Ribbon** list box, click **New Group** to create a group.
5. If necessary, rename a tab or a group.
   a. In the **Customize the Ribbon** list box, select a tab or a group.
   b. Display the **Rename** dialog box.
      - Below the **Customize the Ribbon** list box, click **Rename,** or;
      - Right-click the tab or group and choose **Rename.**
   c. In the **Rename** dialog box, in the **Display name** text box, enter the desired name and click **OK.**
6. Add commands to a group.
   a. In the **Customize the Ribbon** list box, select a group to which you want to add commands.
   b. From the **Choose commands from** drop-down list, select the desired category from which you want to select commands.
   c. In the **Choose commands from** list box, select the desired command that you want to add to the group.
   d. Click **Add** to add the selected command to the selected group on the ribbon.
7. If necessary, in the **Customize the Ribbon** list box, select a command and click **Remove** to remove it.
8. If necessary, in the **Customize the Ribbon** list box, uncheck the check box next to a tab or group to hide it.
9. In the **Outlook Options** dialog box, click **OK.**

Minimizing the Ribbon

Although it is not possible to move or hide the ribbon, you can minimize it so that you will have more space available in your work area. To minimize the ribbon, you can select **Minimize the Ribbon** from the **Customize Quick Access Toolbar** drop-down list. You can also double-click the active tab on the ribbon or press **Ctrl+F1.** The interface will display only the tabs; the corresponding groups and galleries will be hidden. To restore the ribbon, select any of the tabs.

Procedure Reference: Customize the Status Bar

To customize the status bar:

1. Launch the Outlook application.
2. Right-click the status bar.
3. From the **Customize Status Bar** menu, choose the desired options.

> On the **Customize Status Bar** menu, when you choose an option, a check mark is displayed to its left to indicate that the selected option will be displayed on the status bar. Choosing the desired option again hides it.

4. Click away from the **Customize Status Bar** menu to close it.

ACTIVITY 7-1
Customizing the Microsoft Office Outlook User Interface

Scenario:
You want to add frequently used commands such as **Back, Forward,** and **Print** to the Quick Access toolbar to increase your efficiency. You also wish to add the **New** group to the Quick Access toolbar because you frequently use the **New Items** command. You need to customize the ribbon by adding a new tab and a group to it. You also want to change the color scheme of the interface to blue, and customize the status bar to display options according to your preference.

1. Change the color of the Outlook interface to blue.

    a. On the ribbon, select the **File** tab to display the Backstage view.

    b. In the left pane, click **Options** to launch the **Outlook Options** dialog box.

    c. In the **Outlook Options** dialog box, observe that the **General** tab is selected.

    d. In the **User Interface options** section, from the **Color scheme** drop-down list, select **Blue** to change the color of the Outlook interface to blue.

    e. Click **OK** to close the **Outlook Options** dialog box and observe that the color scheme is changed to blue.

2. Add a tab to the ribbon.

    a. Select the **File** tab and choose **Options.**

    b. In the **Outlook Options** dialog box, select the **Customize Ribbon** tab.

    c. In the right pane, below the **Customize the Ribbon** list box, click **New Tab.**

d. Observe that a tab named **New Tab (Custom)** is added to the **Customize the Ribbon** list box.

```
Main Tabs
  ☑ Home (Mail)
      ⊞ New
      ⊞ Delete
      ⊞ Respond
      ⊞ Quick Steps
      ⊞ Move
      ⊞ RSS
      ⊞ Tags
      ⊞ Chinese Conversion
      ⊞ Find
      ⊞ Send/Receive (IMAP/POP)
  ☑ New Tab (Custom)
          New Group (Custom)
  ⊞ ☑ Home (Calendar Table View)
```

3. Add a command to the new Ribbon tab.

   a. In the **Customize the Ribbon** list box, verify that **New Group (Custom)** is selected.

   b. Click **Rename,** and in the **Rename** dialog box, in the **Display name** text box, type *My Group* and click **OK** to change the name of the group.

   c. Similarly, rename the **New Tab (Custom)** tab to *My Tab*

   d. In the **Customize the Ribbon** list box, select **My Group (Custom).**

   e. From the **Choose commands from** drop-down list, select **All Commands** to display all the available commands in the list box.

   f. In the list box, select **Address Book** and click **Add.**

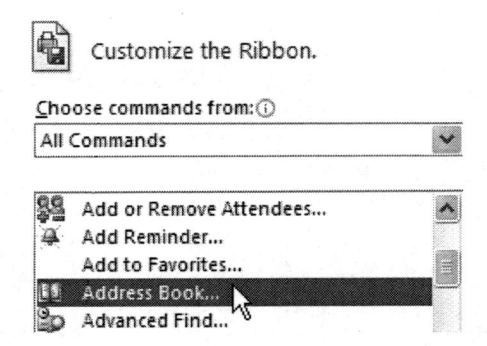

   ```
   Customize the Ribbon.
   Choose commands from:
   [All Commands       ▼]
   
   Add or Remove Attendees...
   Add Reminder...
   Add to Favorites...
   Address Book...
   Advanced Find...
   ```

   g. In the **Choose commands from** list box, scroll down, select **Calendar,** and click **Add.**

   h. Click **OK** to exit the **Outlook Options** dialog box.

   i. On the ribbon, select **My Tab.**

j. Observe that the commands are added to a group named **My Group.**

---

4. Add the **Back, Forward,** and **Print** commands to the Quick Access toolbar.

    a. In the **Outlook Options** dialog box, select **Quick Access Toolbar.**

    b. Observe that in the **Choose commands from** drop-down list, **Popular Commands** is selected.

    c. In the **Choose commands from** list box, select **Back.**

    d. Click **Add** to add the **Back** button to the Quick Access toolbar.

    e. In the **Choose commands from** list box, select **Forward** and then click **Add.**

    f. In the list box, select **Print** and then click **Add.**

    g. In the **Customize Quick Access toolbar** list box, observe that the **Print** command is selected and click the **Move Up** button to move the **Print** command one step above in the order.

    > The **Move Up** button is located to the right of the list box.

    h. Click **OK** to close the **Outlook Options** dialog box.

    i. Observe that the added commands are displayed on the Quick Access toolbar.

---

5. Add the **New** group to the Quick Access toolbar.

    a. On the **Home** tab, in the **New** group, below the buttons, right-click the word **New** and choose **Add to Quick Access Toolbar.**

    b. On the Quick Access toolbar, click the **New** button to display the options in the **New** group.

Lesson 7: Customizing the Outlook Environment   177

c. On the **Home** tab of the ribbon, observe that all the options in the **New** group are now accessible from the Quick Access toolbar.

d. Click the **New** button again to close the **New** group.

6. Customize the status bar to remove the display of the **Zoom Slider, Zoom,** and **Filter** items.

   a. Right-click anywhere on the status bar to view the menu options.

   b. Observe that a check mark is displayed next to the **Items in View** denoting that the status bar will display the item being viewed.

   c. From the displayed menu, choose **Zoom Slider** to remove the display of the zoom slider from the status bar.

   d. Select **Zoom** to remove the display of the zoom percentage from the status bar.

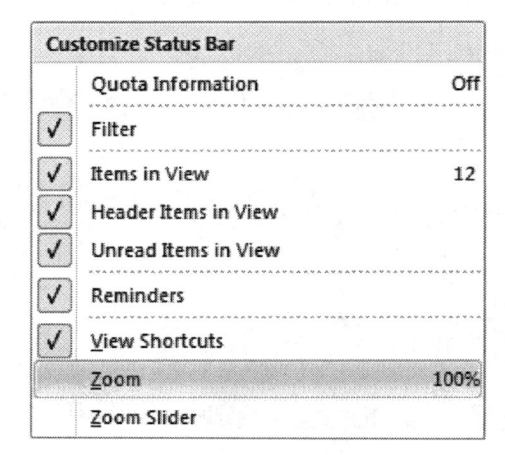

Customize Status Bar	
Quota Information	Off
✓ Filter	
✓ Items in View	12
✓ Header Items in View	
✓ Unread Items in View	
✓ Reminders	
✓ View Shortcuts	
Zoom	100%
Zoom Slider	

   e. Select **Filter** to avoid displaying filter information on the status bar.

   f. On the status bar, click the empty area to the left of the menu to close the menu.

TOPIC B
Customize the To-Do Bar

You have customized the ribbon and the Quick Access toolbar to suit your workflow. You may now want to organize the To-Do bar, so you can easily keep track of your daily tasks. In this topic, you will customize the To-Do bar.

You use a shopping list to remember what you need to buy when you go to a store. Similarly, you can refer to the To-Do bar to see upcoming events you have to attend and messages that you have flagged. Customizing the To-Do bar will help you to organize the items you need and turn off the rest. You can also reposition items on the To-Do bar to suit your own priorities.

How to Customize the To-Do Bar

Procedure Reference: Customize the View and Components of the To-Do Bar

To customize the view and components of the To-Do bar:

1. Display a folder.
2. Expand the To-Do bar.
   - In the top-right corner of the To-Do bar, click the **Expand the To-Do Bar** button, or;
   - On the **View** tab, in the **Layout** group, choose **To-Do Bar→Normal** to expand the To-Do bar.
3. Customize the components of the To-Do bar.
   - Arrange calendars in the To-Do bar.
     - To show more calendars arranged horizontally in the To-Do bar, drag the dividing line between the Reading pane and the To-Do Bar to increase or decrease the width of the To-Do bar. When you release the mouse button, the number of calendars will increase or decrease to fill the available space.
     - To show more calendars arranged vertically in the To-Do bar, use the **To-Do Bar Options** dialog box.
       a. On the To-Do bar, right-click and choose **Options.**
       b. Under the **Show Date Navigator** section, in the **Number of month rows** text box, type a number from 0 to 9 to display the calendars vertically in the specified rows.
   - Customize the display of appointments in the To-Do bar.
     a. Display the **To-Do Bar Options** dialog box.
     b. Under the **Show Appointments** section, check the **Show All Day Events** and **Show Details of Private Items** check boxes that need to be displayed.
   - In the **To-Do Bar Options** dialog box, hide the To-Do bar components that you do not want to display.
     - Uncheck the **Show Date Navigator** check box to hide the Date Navigator.
     - Uncheck the **Show Appointments** check box to hide the appointments.
     - Uncheck the **Show Task List** check box to hide the Task list.
   - View more tasks in the Task list of the To-Do bar.

- Turn off the Date Navigator.
- Change the number of appointments that are displayed.

• Click the **Minimize the To-Do Bar** button to minimize or restore the To-Do bar on the top-right corner of the To-Do bar pane.

• Hide or display the To-Do bar.
  - On the **View** tab, in the **Layout** group, choose **To-Do Bar→Off** to hide the To-Do bar.
  - On the **View** tab, in the **Layout** group, choose **To-Do Bar→Minimized** to display the To-Do bar again.

> The To-Do bar is turned on by default. It can also be turned on or off by pressing **Alt+ F2**.

ACTIVITY 7-2
Customizing the To-Do bar

Scenario:
As a manager, you receive multiple meeting requests every day. Therefore, you want to customize your To-Do bar so that it reflects your personal preferences. You want to display the calendars for the current month and the next three months on your To-Do bar so that when you click any time slot, you can quickly view all the appointments, meetings, and events happening in those months.

1. Customize the Calendar view in the To-Do bar.

    a. Display the **Inbox** folder.

    b. On the **View** tab, in the **Layout** group, choose **To-Do Bar→Normal** to expand the To-Do bar.

    c. Click and drag the dividing line between the Reading pane and the To-Do bar to the left of the screen to display the next month's calendar.

    d. On the **View** tab, in the **Layout** group, choose **To-Do Bar→Options** to display the **To-Do Bar Options** dialog box.

    e. In the **Show Date Navigator** section, in the **Number of month rows** text box, triple-click and type *2*

    f. Click **OK** to display the calendars vertically in two rows.

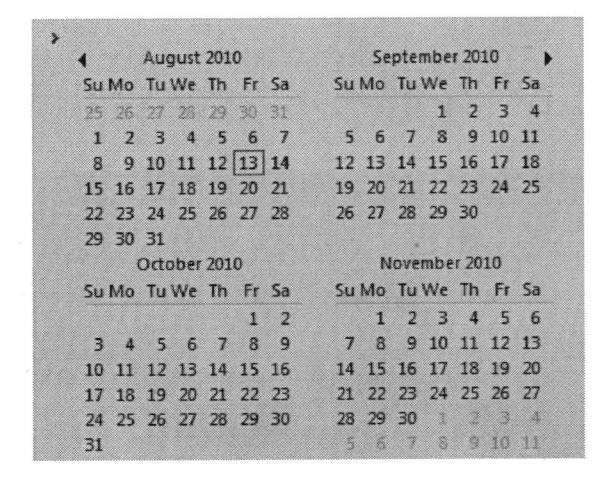

2. Hide the Task list.

Lesson 7: Customizing the Outlook Environment 181

Microsoft® Office Outlook® 2010: Level 2

    a.   On the **View** tab, in the **Layout** group, choose **To-Do Bar→Options** to display the **To-Do Bar Options** dialog box.

    b.   Uncheck the **Show Task List** check box and click **OK** to hide the Task list.

    c.   Observe that the Task list has been removed from the To-Do bar.

Lesson 7: Customizing the Outlook Environment

TOPIC C
Create a Folder Home Page

You have customized the To-Do bar to keep track of what you need to do. Just as you refer to your To-Do bar for tasks, you may frequently refer to a particular web page for information. In this topic, you will create a folder home page so that you can display the web page without having to open it in a browser.

As part of your day-to-day activities, you may frequently visit a particular web page. Every time you need to reference the page, you have to open a web browser, and then the page. Outlook allows you to display a web page in a folder so that you can refer to it whenever you want.

The Folder Home Page

A *folder home page* is a local, Intranet, or Internet web page that is associated with an Outlook folder. It is displayed when the folder is opened, making it convenient and easy to access information without having to leave Outlook. Every Outlook folder supports a folder home page.

Figure 7-1: The folder home page displaying a web page.

How to Create a Folder Home Page

Procedure Reference: Assign a Home Page to a Folder

To assign a folder home page to an Outlook folder:

1. Select an existing folder or create a new folder.
2. Right-click the folder that you want to assign a folder home page, and choose **Properties**.
3. In the [Folder name] **Properties** dialog box, select the **Home Page** tab.
4. In the **Address** text box, type the URL of the website that you want to set as the default home page for the new folder.

> You can also navigate to the address.

> You can choose a local folder home page that maps to a file that might change frequently, enabling you to view updates when you click the folder. Follow the same procedure for creating a home page; however, use the **Browse** button on the **Home Page** tab of the **Folder Properties** dialog box to locate and select the file.

5. Check the **Show home page by default for this folder** check box to set the web page to open when you click the folder.
6. Click **OK** to close the dialog box.

ACTIVITY 7-3
Assigning a Folder Home Page

Before You Begin:
Display the **Inbox** folder.

Scenario:
You see that there are a lot of updates happening in your website, **ourglobalcompany.com**, and keeping track of them is becoming increasingly cumbersome. Therefore, in order to keep abreast of daily updates, you want to add the website as a folder home page for your Our Global Company folder.

1. Create a folder called **Our Global Company** in your Inbox.

    a. In the Navigation pane, right-click the **Inbox** folder and choose **New Folder.**

    b. In the **Create New Folder** dialog box, in the **Name** text box, type *Our Global Company* and click **OK** to create a folder named **Our Global Company** under your **Inbox** folder.

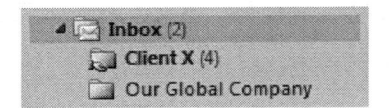

2. Specify a home page for the subfolder.

    a. In the Navigation pane, right-click the **Our Global Company** folder and choose **Properties.**

    b. In the **Our Global Company Properties** dialog box, select the **Home Page** tab.

    c. In the **Address** text box, type *http://www.ourglobalcompany.com*

    d. Check the **Show home page by default for this folder** check box and click **OK** to close the dialog box.

    e. In the Navigation pane, select the **Our Global Company** folder to display the Our Global Company home page as the default home page for this folder.

Lesson 7 Follow-up

In this lesson, you customized the Outlook environment. By customizing the environment, you can arrange the toolbar, ribbon, and other commands to suit your needs and preferences.

1. **What modifications are you likely to make to the Outlook environment?**

2. **Is there a command that you use frequently and requires multiple steps to execute, but which you could access more easily through customization?**

Follow-up

In this course, you have tracked work activities, shared folders, assigned and tracked tasks, and quickly located Outlook items. You have also customized the Outlook environment to suit your preferences. Now, you have the opportunity to set up Outlook to reflect your needs and preferences.

1. **What types of activities might you track using the Outlook Journal?**

2. **To what level, will customizing the Outlook environment help the end user?**

3. **What do you consider to be the biggest advantage of using Outlook 2010? Why?**

What's Next?

This course is the second in a series of three Microsoft Outlook courses. *Microsoft® Office Outlook® 2010: Level 3* is the next course in the series.

Lesson Labs

Lesson labs are provided as an additional learning resource for this course. The labs may or may not be performed as part of the classroom activities. Your instructor will consider setup issues, classroom timing issues, and instructional needs to determine which labs are appropriate for you to perform, and at what point during the class. If you do not perform the labs in class, your instructor can tell you if you can perform them independently as self-study, and if there are any special setup requirements.

Lesson 1 Lab 1
Setting Message Options

Activity Time: 20 minutes

Scenario:
After checking your calendar for tomorrow, you discover that you have a 6:30-PM dinner meeting with a colleague you used to work with. You're certain that your partner and a few other colleagues would also enjoy seeing this old friend. You want to invite them all, and because you frequently send items to this group, you will create a distribution list called "Old HR Group" that includes your partner and two other coworkers. Due to the timeliness and nature of the message, it has a high level of importance and needs to remain private. In case the recipients don't open the message tomorrow before close of business, you set the message to expire at that time.

1. Create a contact group, **Old HR Group**, that includes your partner and two other users of your choice.

2. Create and address a new message to **Old HR Group**, inviting them to dinner.

3. Set a high importance level and a private sensitivity level.

4. Set the necessary delivery option so that the message will expire if unopened by tomorrow at 5:00 PM.

5. Send the message.

Lesson 2 Lab 1
Organizing and Locating Items

Activity Time: 20 minutes

1. Send a mail to your partner with the subject "System Training" and the message body "Hi Susan Jones, Please let me know when an interview can be scheduled. Thanks."

Scenario:

You need to organize your messages and locate an email containing a reference to Susan Jones. You also need to find the messages sent to the Applicants contact group

1. Sort your Inbox messages by importance in ascending order, and then by size, with the largest files appearing first in the list.

2. Find any email message that contains the text "Susan Jones."

3. Display all messages in the Inbox folder list.

4. Clear the filter.

Lesson 3 Lab 1
Setting Calendar Options

Activity Time: 20 minutes

Scenario:

Due to a company reorganization, your department has moved to Hawaii and you need to change your calendar to reflect the new time zone. Due to the increase in the number of team members, you need to add their calendars to form a calendar group for easy scheduling of meetings. In addition, your workdays and hours have changed to Monday through Friday, 9:00 AM to 5:00 PM.

1. Change your main calendar to the Hawaii time zone.

2. Add a new calendar group containing the calendars of your team members.

3. Change your work week to reflect the new schedule.

Lesson 4 Lab 1
Keeping Track of Work Activities Using the Journal

Activity Time: 20 minutes

Objective:
Track work activities using the Journal.

Scenario:
You want to use the Journal to track an email message you must send to your partner, as well as to manually record a Journal entry for the time you spent in going out to purchase a cartridge.

1. Display the Outlook Journal, and set it to automatically record all Outlook items, as well as any items that pertain to your partner.

2. Send an email to your partner with a subject and message of your choice.

3. Open and verify the Journal Entry form for the message sent in step 2.

4. Manually record and save a Journal entry, with details of your choice, for a visit to the office supply store to pick up a printer cartridge.

5. Turn off the Journal feature.

Lesson 5 Lab 1
Managing Your Work

Activity Time: 20 minutes

Scenario:
The booth for the job expo needs some minor carpentry work. As the Job Expo coordinator, you need to create a task request and assign this task to your partner, who accepts it. After a week of progress, your partner wants to notify you of its status, and sends a task update stating that the project is 75 percent complete and should finish early.

1. Create a task request addressed to your partner regarding the repair of the expo booth.

2. Mark the task a high priority with a due date of two weeks from today.

3. Assign the task to the Job Expo category.

4. Send the task request.

5. Once the task request is received, accept the expo booth repair task request from your partner.

6. Send a task update informing the originator that the task is 75 percent complete.

Microsoft® Office Outlook® 2010: Level 2

Lesson 6 Lab 1
Sharing Outlook Information

Activity Time: 20 minutes

Objective:
Share Outlook information.

Setup:
Your assigned partner is also performing this practice activity.

Scenario:
You are going on a two-week business trip and need to assign your partner as a delegate, with Owner permission, to your Calendar folder. As a delegate to your partner's Calendar folder, you access your partner's calendar, schedule a one-hour dentist appointment, and then close the calendar.

Also, in your contacts list, the company name for one of your contacts, Eve Alexander, needs to be specified as Our Global Company. You have assigned your partner as a delegate, with an Editor permission level, to your Contacts folder.

1. Delegate access to your Calendar folder to your partner, assigning Owner-level permission.

2. Access your partner's calendar and schedule a one-hour dentist appointment for three weeks from today, with a time of your choice.

3. Close your partner's calendar.

4. Verify that the dentist appointment has been added to your calendar.

5. Send your calendar information to your partner through email.

6. Delegate access to your Contacts folder to your partner, assigning Editor-level permission.

7. Access your partner's Contacts folder and update the contact information of Eve Alexander.

Lesson 7 Lab 1
Customizing the Outlook Interface

Activity Time: 20 minutes

Scenario:

In an attempt to work more efficiently, you want to add the Undo button to the ribbon and the Distribution List command as an option under the My Menu choice. Also, you want to add the Meeting Request button to the Quick Access toolbar and display the calendars for the next six months on the To-Do bar. Finally, to keep yourself posted on daily updates, you decide to add the **http://citizensinfo.com** website as a folder home page for your Training Site folder.

1. Add the Undo button to the ribbon under a group named My Menu.

2. Add the New Contact Group command option under the My Menu choice.

3. Add the Meeting Request button to the Quick Access toolbar in a location of your choice.

4. Customize the To-Do bar to display the calendars for the next six months.

5. Create a folder named Training Site and set its home page as **http://www.citizensinfo.org**

Solutions

Lesson 1

Activity 1-1

5. **True or False? You can view the message sensitivity level in the message InfoBar.**

    ✓ True

    ___ False

6. **True or False? When you forward a message, you can remove the importance setting but not the sensitivity setting.**

    ___ True

    ✓ False

Activity 1-4

2. **True or False? In a Message window, text formatting options, such as bold and italic, are available on the Options tab.**

    ___ True

    ✓ False

Activity 1-5

5. **What happens when you send a message to someone who has turned on the Automatic Replies?**

    a) The message sits in your Outbox folder until the individual returns.

    ✓ b) The message is sent and you are alerted to the fact that the recipient is out of office.

    c) The message is returned to your Inbox folder.

    d) The message sits in your Drafts folder until the individual returns.

Microsoft® Office Outlook® 2010: Level 2

Activity 1-7

2. True or False? Within the To text box of the email message, Contact Groups are preceded by a plus sign icon.

    ✓ True
    __ False

Lesson 2

Activity 2-1

2. True or False? Messages are listed in alphabetical or numerical order by senders' user names. For each sender, messages are listed in the order they were received, with the newest messages listed at the top.

    ✓ True
    __ False

Activity 2-3

3. True or False? Items that contain the word "resume" and have a high importance level are displayed at the bottom of the Advanced Find window.

    ✓ True
    __ False

Activity 2-5

3. True or False? Messages that satisfy the specified criteria are displayed in the Sent Items folder list.

    ✓ True
    __ False

Lesson 3

Activity 3-2

2. True or False? You can edit the Time zone option in Outlook to view a different time zone instead of the current one.

    __ True
    ✓ False

Activity 3-3

2. True or False? You can update the free/busy information on the server in Outlook.
   - ✓ True
   - ___ False

Activity 3-4

2. Which function can be performed by a Calendar group?
   - a) Export a Calendar
   - b) View Calendar holidays
   - c) Set availability options
   - ✓ d) View Calendars side by side

Activity 3-5

2. True or False? You can move the responses only to your Inbox.
   - ___ True
   - ✓ False

Lesson 4

Activity 4-1

3. True or False? When you first turn a Journal on, there are Journal entries already recorded in it.
   - ___ True
   - ✓ False

Activity 4-2

3. What is true about the Improved Process Call Journal entry displayed in the journal?
   - ✓ a) It is represented by an icon of a telephone.
   - b) It identifies contact information.
   - ✓ c) It is displayed under an expanded Phone Call entry type.
   - d) It displays the duration of the activity.

Lesson 6

Activity 6-1

2. **When granting permissions to your Inbox, you must:**
   - ✓ a) Set a delegate name
   - ✓ b) Assign permission roles
   - ✓ c) Assign level of access
   -    d) Deny permission roles

Activity 6-2

3. **True or False? In the Side-By-Side mode, your partner's calendar is displayed beside your calendar and a new check box for displaying or hiding the shared calendar is displayed in the Navigation pane.**
   - ✓ True
   -     False

Glossary

actions
The tasks to be performed when a set of conditions are met.

Arrangement group
A group of items that displays your emails in a your view preference.

Automatic Replies
A tool that enables you to perform actions by applying rules and automatically send replies when you are out of office.

calendar group
An option in the Calendar view that allows you to place calendars of users in a group, so as to compare their schedules before you schedule a meeting.

conditions
The characteristics to be checked in an incoming message.

contact group
A collection of user names referred to by one unique name. It is used to address an email message to multiple users easily.

delegate
A delegate is a person who has been given permission to access someone else's Outlook folders.

Delivery options
A set of options that allow you to change the way Outlook delivers your message.

delivery receipt
A message notification that confirms that your message was delivered to its intended recipients.

filter
A procedure used to display the items that meet specified conditions only.

folder home page
A web page that appears in an Outlook folder whenever the folder is opened.

HTML
(Hypertext Markup Language) A message format that supports text formatting, numbering, bullets, alignment, pictures, HTML styles, and hyperlinks.

hyperlink
An object, text, or graphic that links to another location.

Instant Search
Allows you to search for items in Outlook.

Journal
An Outlook feature that automatically records actions that you perform and displays them in various timeline views.

Junk E-Mail Filter
A filter that automatically checks every incoming message to determine whether it is a suspicious or fraudulent email.

message format
A way of encoding a message that determines the type of formatting applied to a message and how it is displayed.

message settings
Settings that inform the recipient of the importance and sensitivity of a message.

permission role
Specifies the level of access that another person can have to one of your folders.

plain text
A text-only message format that does not support pictures, bold and italic formatting, colored fonts, and other text formatting.

Query Builder
A feature that provides multiple search fields to make your search more focused.

quick step
A command that facilitates performing common tasks that involve multiple actions as a single click option.

read receipt
A message notification that confirms that the recipient has read your message.

RTF
(Rich Text Format) A message format that supports text formatting, bullets, alignment, pictures, and linked objects.

rule
A set of conditions and the corresponding actions to be performed when the conditions are met.

Rules Wizard
A series of dialog boxes that take you step-by-step through the process of creating a rule. These rules are made of a condition and an action.

Send Status Report
A detailed email that contains details such as Status, % complete, and the Actual work hours spent on the task.

sort criteria
The categories by which a list of items can be sorted.

spam
Unsolicited email advertising for a product that is sent to an individual, mailing list, or newsgroup.

Task Request form
A form that enables you to request updates and status reports on the progress of a task as well as to delegate a task to another user.

Index

A

Arrangement group, 67
automatic meeting responses
 generating, 107

C

calendar groups, 105
 creating, 105
calendars
 adding holidays to, 93
 displaying an additional time zone, 98
 setting workdays and time, 93
 viewing in Overlay mode, 155
Conditional Formatting, 68
conditions
 and actions for automatic replies, 20
contact groups, 27
 creating, 28
 modifying, 28
contextual tabs
 Search Tools, 48

D

delegates, 162
delivery options, 10
 modifying, 12
delivery receipts, 11
dialog boxes
 Advanced Find, 55
 Automatic Replies, 19
 Filter, 62
 Free/Busy Options, 101
 Manage Quick Steps, 38
 Outlook Options, 92
 Send A Calendar via E-mail, 158

F

feedback gathering, 3
filters, 62
 clearing, 64
 for junk email, 83
folder home pages, 183
folder permissions
 specifying, 151
folders, 149
 accessing other users', 155
 Junk E-Mail, 86

H

hyperlinks, 34
 characteristics of, 34
 inserting in messages, 35

I

Instant Search, 48
 search for items using, 50
Internet calendars
 subscribing to, 93
 Also See: Overlay mode

J

Journal, 114
journal entries
 modifying, 123
 recording automatically, 116
 recording manually, 120
Journal Entry forms, 119
Journal views, 115

L

lists

Blocked Senders, 84
Safe Senders, 84
Update, 139

M

message formats, 15
  specifying for an individual's message, 17
  types of, 16
message forwarding
  without the high importance flag, 4
message settings, 2
  modifying, 4
  types of, 2
messages
  filtering, 64
  marking as not junk, 86
  organizing, 70
  sorting, 45
  using a rule to delete, 71
  using a rule to forward, 73
  using criteria to find, 56

O

options
  Time zones, 97
out of office notifications
  setting, 21
Overlay mode, 154

P

permission roles, 148
  and levels, 148

Q

Query Builder, 54
  using to find items, 56
Quick Access toolbar
  customizing, 172
quick steps, 37
  creating, 39

R

read receipts, 11
reply options, 134
ribbon
  customizing, 173
  minimizing, 174
rules, 20
  deleting, 74
Rules Wizard, 68

S

sort criteria, 44
sorts
  types of, 44
spam, 83
status bar
  customizing, 174
status options, 129
status reports, 139

T

tabs
  Calendar, 92
  Search, 49
Task Request forms, 128
task updates
  sending, 140
tasks
  assigning, 129
  marking the status as deferred, 140
  tracking, 142
To-Do bar
  customizing, 179

V

voting buttons, 3
  Also See: feedback gathering
  creating messages with, 4